1980

Directors: Myth and Reality

Directors: Myth and Reality

MYLES L. MACE
Professor of Business Administration
Harvard University

DIVISION OF RESEARCH
GRADUATE SCHOOL OF BUSINESS ADMINISTRATION
HARVARD UNIVERSITY

Boston • 1971

Second printing June 1972

Library of Congress Catalog Card No. 79-168849
ISBN 0-87584-094-9

Printed in the United States of America

PREFACE

ONE of the privileges of a faculty member of the Harvard Business School is the opportunity to be relieved from classroom responsibilities so that he can concentrate his full energies on a research topic of his choice. This I have done during the last two and a half years.

The chance to study and report on what boards of directors in fact do fills a gap in business literature and, I hope, establishes a basis upon which responsible leadership can evolve new concepts and new roles for boards of directors. Almost all the business leaders whom I interviewed share concerns about the workings of boards of directors and are searching for new and better answers.

The basic data for a research project of this sort were accumulated from personal interviews. To all the executives and directors who shared their time, experience, and examples illustrating their conclusions I am deeply indebted. An explicit condition of all interviews was that our conversations were confidential and that real names of people and companies would not be used in whatever was published. With this assurance top executives talked openly and freely, not only about the boards and board members of their own companies, but also about board members and boards where they served as outside directors. Acknowledgment by name is obviously precluded, but those interviewed will find themselves in these pages.

The research was initiated when Dean Lawrence E. Fouraker was the Director of Research. His encouragement and the support of Dean Fouraker's successor as Director of

Research, Professor Richard E. Walton, with Professor James P. Baughman, Associate Director of Research, provided the ideal administrative conditions for what I wanted to do. Financial support for this research project came from an allocation of funds from gifts to the School by The Associates of the Harvard Business School.

Colleagues and former colleagues as well maintained continuous interest in the project and contributed invaluable perceptions and suggestions. Among these were Professors Melvin T. Copeland, Edmund P. Learned, Kenneth R. Andrews, Robert W. Austin, M. Colyer Crum, Bertrand Fox, Eli Shapiro (now Chairman of the Finance Committee, The Travelers Insurance Company, Hartford), Dan T. Smith, and Michael von Clemm.

Highly competent typing and secretarial help was provided by Mrs. Katherine C. Griffith, Miss Camilla Moon, and Miss Lorna Slocombe, who in addition to doing the tedious typing from tapes made editorial suggestions.

Miss Ruth Norton, Editor and Executive Secretary of the Division of Research, requires a special acknowledgment. This volume is the fourth manuscript for which I have enjoyed the professional interest and help of Ruth Norton. As before, her suggestions on organization structure and clarity of expression were gently, perceptively, and constructively made.

The years devoted to this research project required and received my complete interest and involvement. The top priority of travel, interviews, and writing necessarily resulted in adjustments in our normal household patterns. My wife, Adelaide "Bunny" Rowley Mace, cheerfully accommodated to whatever was needed, and when in writing I struggled with a particularly perplexing section she was there to talk about the problem and to help work out a new approach. She read every chapter of the first longhand draft

of the manuscript, and her devotion to completing the research and the manuscript was no less than mine.

The responsibility for the conduct of the study and for
the report rests inevitably on the author.

MYLES L. MACE

JUNE 1971

CONTENTS

Directors: Myth and Reality

CHAPTER I

Introduction

MY interest in boards of directors and board activities goes back to 1946 when Professor Melvin T. Copeland —"Doc" to his friends and associates—encouraged me to complete the requirements for the doctor's degree at the Harvard Business School. Our discussions led to the identification of a need for a study of the boards of directors of small corporations. This need, coupled with my involvement in starting a new course on small business, "The Management of New Enterprises," resulted in a study and a dissertation, *The Board of Directors in Small Corporations,* which was published by the Business School's Division of Research in 1948.

Small corporations, as well as large and medium-sized corporations, are legal entities chartered under state business corporation laws, which generally provide that "The business of a corporation shall be managed by a board of at least three directors." In that early study of what "shall be managed" meant in small corporations, it became apparent very early in the inquiry that the typical corporate board of directors was largely a vestigial legal organ which included merely subservient and docile appointees of the owner-manager. Obviously such a board did not participate in the management of the business, but it did meet the letter of the law by having certain persons designated as members of the board. I found also that active and able board members constituted a source of management assistance to small corporation managements, and that this source of help could be tapped for advice and counsel on any problems involved in the operations of the business. The extent to which the boards were effective depended largely on the desires of the small corporation managements—their desires to include competent men on their boards, and their desires to take advantage of board members' advice and counsel.

My interest in the functions of boards of directors has continued over these intervening years. I have served on the boards of several large and medium-sized companies, compiled notes on my observations, and interviewed informally literally hundreds of top corporate executives and directors. My own experiences on boards, and the experiences of those interviewed, began to indicate a considerable gap between what professors and business executives have stated boards of directors should do and what in fact they do. As I watched board members and company presidents in action, I wondered whether boards of large and medium-sized companies fulfilled functions different from those of the boards of small corporations.

With mounting evidence of a considerable gap between the academic or legal definition of board functions, and what boards actually do; with a search of the literature turning up nothing on the subject of what boards of directors really do; encouraged by executives to undertake a research study of the problem; stimulated by expressions of concern from the various publics of business corporations; and disregarding my self-imposed resolution that I had written my last book—I outlined a plan of research to the then Director of Research at the Harvard Business School, Professor Lawrence E. Fouraker. The program was approved, and this, my last book, is the product.

METHODOLOGY

Since 1948 when I completed the research process and writing for my doctoral dissertation, I estimate that I have

spent several thousand hours in board meetings and working and consulting outside of board meetings with company
top managements on board problems. This background
provided the basis for the construction of the working hy-
potheses employed during the last two years of concentrated
and intensive field research interviews. What would com-
prise an adequate additional sample for a study like this
was hard to define. I found that after about seventy-five
interviews in depth, and several hundred shorter discussions
with executives, a pattern was apparent. I concluded that
more interviews would add little of incremental value.

Thus this was not a statistical study dependent upon ques-
tionnaries filled out by corporate respondents. I believed
that this approach would result in misleading and fallacious
conclusions. It is easy for a board member to apply self-
serving and conscience-salving descriptive phrases to his own
perception of his role as a responsible director. It is more
difficult for him to describe his role and support conclusions
with evidence while he is being interviewed by an interested and reasonably experienced student of business
practice.

Some of the interviews were recorded on tape. They
usually lasted from two to six hours. Other interviews consisted of verbally recounted experiences and illustrations,
and I have tried to maintain the integrity of these comments through my subsequent notes. Many executives preferred not to have their comments recorded in any form.
One said, "What I have to say about boards of directors
should never be in writing and associated with my name."
Every interviewee was assured that our conversation was
completely confidential, that nothing would be written
which would be embarrassing to any persons or companies,
and that when the results were published, all names of
people, companies, industries, and locations would be disguised. Without this assurance to those who so willingly
shared their experiences and observations, this study would

not have been possible. My interest, and I am sure also the interest of those who participated in this project, is to make a contribution to a better understanding of that layer of management organization known as the board of directors.

Before proceeding further I wish to note the following limitations. This study is concerned for the most part with boards of directors in large and medium-sized, widely held companies in which the president and the directors own little common or other voting stock. Instances are included, however, where directors own or represent the ownership of large stock interests. The effect on the behavior of directors with substantial stock ownership or the representatives of substantial stock ownership is reported in Chapters III, IV, and VIII.

Also, this study is confined to the boards of directors of manufacturing, mining, and re ailing companies. Financial institutions, banks, insurance companies, trust companies, transportation companies, and utility companies have been excluded.

In this report I use the title "president" to mean the chief executive officer, recognizing that in some corporations the chief executive officer may have the title, "chairman of the board."

LEGAL HISTORY

Business corporations and boards of directors have been part of the business scene for at least 150 years in the United States, and even longer in England. "In the year 1553," for example, "a group of London merchants financed an exploratory voyage by Sebastian Cabot, the son of John Cabot, for the purpose of opening up trade relations with the Russians through the port of Archangel. When one of the three original vessels returned safely to England with a report that the Russians were receptive, the London merchants obtained from Bloody Mary a royal charter as a corporation 'as one bodie and perpetuall fellowship and commaltie' known as the 'Russia Company' or, more extensively, as the 'Merchant Adventurers of England for the Discovery of Lands, Territories, Isles, Dominions and Seignories, unknown and not before that late adventure or enterprise by sea or navigation commonly frequented.' This was the first English Company intended to operate on a joint stock."[1]

This concept—that the privilege of operating in the joint stock or corporate form was possible only by a grant from the Crown—was adopted later by the colonies and individual states in America. In the early 1800s state legislatures voted special charters to a variety of enterprises. "In 1818, for example, Massachusetts chartered the Maine Flour Mills, but limited the total property which they might hold to $50,000, of which they might hold land not to exceed $30,000 in value, and it had to be in Kennebec County."[2]

Inevitably the negotiations between political leaders, enterprisers, and key persons in state capitals led to maneuvering and corruption, with the result that legislators concluded that "special charters (the only kind theretofore known) were inherently bad; that the privilege of doing business as a corporation ought to be available to anyone and, by consequence, that states should have a general incorporation law permitting any business group which fulfills its formalities to obtain a charter from the state. . . . The privilege of doing business as a corporation thus be-

---

[1] Dow Votaw, "The Politics of a Changing Corporate Society," *California Management Review*, Spring 1960, p. 106.

[2] Adolf A. Berle, Jr., "Historical Inheritance of American Corporations," Section 1 of Introduction, William L. Cary, *Cases and Materials on Corporations*, Mineola, The Foundation Press, 4th ed., 1969, p. 3. This introduction, pp. 1–5, provides a good brief historical background.

came generally available. . . . The first 'general corporation law for business purposes' is commonly credited to the State of New York, in the year 1811. . . . By 1900 not only were general incorporation laws practically universal, but many states had included clauses in their state constitutions forbidding the granting of special charters."[3]

The general corporation laws adopted by the states typically provide that the management of the enterprise is the responsibility of the board of directors—"the business of a corporation shall be managed by a board of at least three directors . . ."[4] or that "the business of every corporation shall be managed and conducted by a president [and] a board of not less than three directors. . . ."[5] But a review of the legal literature and legal cases does not indicate clearly what the functions of directors are, beyond the broad general description that they "shall manage." Hundreds of judicial opinions have been written on legal issues involving directors, but out of these it is impossible to construct any coherent and consistent statement as to what directors' functions actually are.

DEFINITIONS OF DIRECTORS' ROLES

Business literature is replete with the efforts of businessmen, lawyers, and scholars to define the proper and appropriate roles of board members. These writings usually consist of somewhat less general descriptions of the functions of directors than "shall manage," but they are still sufficiently broad so as not to be particularly helpful to a director seeking guidance as to his proper role. A National Industrial

---

[3] *Ibid.*, p. 4.

[4] Minnesota General Laws, Chapter 300, Section 27.

[5] Massachusetts General Laws, Chapter 156, Business Corporations, Section 21.

Conference Board report, for example, lists seven areas of responsibility that appear to have general acceptance:

1. To establish the basic objectives and broad policies of the corporation.
2. To elect the corporate officers, advise them, approve their actions, and audit their performance.
3. To safeguard, and to approve changes in, the corporate assets (issuance of securities, pledge of asset for loans, declaration of dividends, and conveyance of property).
4. To approve important financial decisions and actions (such as budgets, capital appropriations, officers' compensation, and financial audits), and to see that proper annual and interim reports are given to stockholders.
5. To delegate special powers to others to sign contracts, open bank accounts, sign checks, issue stock, make loans, and perform such other activities as may require board approval.
6. To maintain, revise, and enforce the corporate charter and by-laws.
7. To assure maintenance of a sound board through regular elections and filling of interim vacancies.[6]

Melvin T. Copeland and Andrew R. Towl, writing in 1947, described the directors' job as the selection of executives, policy making, checking up on results, and asking discerning questions.[7] And more recently Professor Harold Koontz identified ten major areas in which any board should function[8]—areas generally coincident with those named by the NICB report cited above.

---

[6] *Corporate Directorship Practices,* Joint Report from National Industrial Conference Board and American Society of Corporate Secretaries, Studies in Business Policy, No. 125, New York, 1967, pp. 93–94.
[7] Melvin T. Copeland and Andrew R. Towl, *The Board of Directors and Business Management,* Boston, Division of Research, Harvard Business School, July 1947; reprint, New York, Greenwood Press, 1968.
[8] Harold Koontz, *The Board of Directors and Effective Management,* New York, McGraw-Hill Book Company, 1967, p. 57.

Questions Raised

The law says that the board of directors "manages," and the business literature articulates many particular management responsibilities. But are the law and the business literature merely a part of mythology—beliefs that in this instance do not bear much resemblance to reality? As a participant on, and observer of, boards of directors for over twenty-five years, I have developed a healthy skepticism about the prevailing concept of the board of directors. Specifically, it seemed important to ask what directors actually do in fulfillment of their responsibilities:

1. What is a board of directors like?
2. What does it do?
   Does it provide advice and counsel for the management?
   Does it serve as a disciplinary body?
   Does it select a new president in crisis situations?
3. Does it perform the generally accepted roles of:
   Determining company objectives and strategies?
   Making major company policy decisions?
   Asking discerning questions?
   Selecting the president?
4. What factors determine what directors do?
5. Who holds the powers of control?
6. Do directors represent stockholders?
7. Who are the outside directors, and why do they serve?
8. Should there be insiders on the board?
9. Should members of service organizations, such as investment banking firms, commercial bankers, or legal counsel serve as directors?
10. Is the role of the board of directors in a family-controlled company different?

It was the purpose of this study to find answers to these critically important questions. The chapters that follow report what I found in the course of my research on corporate boards of directors.

CHAPTER II

The Functions of a
Typical Board

W<small>HAT</small> does the board of directors actually do? What has the hundred-year-old language of the incorporation statutes—"the board shall consist of at least three members and shall manage the company"—come through practice to mean today?

A typical board of a large or medium-sized, widely held company, with the president and directors owning little if any common stock, consists of fifteen directors, eight of whom are outsiders and seven are insiders.[1] The inside group includes the chairman, the president, an executive vice president or two, and, depending upon the form of organization, functional vice presidents or divisional vice presidents, and general managers. The outsiders are chairmen and presidents of well-known companies, commercial banks, and insurance companies, and there seems to be a direct relationship between the size of the company represented and the size of the company served as board member. Also the outside director group may include a partner of an investment banking firm, a retired former officer of the company,[2] a partner of the company's retained outside legal counsel, and an educator—usually a university presi-

---

[1] NICB, *Corporate Directorship Practices*, pp. 2, 6–7.

[2] There is considerable discrepancy as to whether former officers continuing on boards are considered insiders or outsiders. Statistics on inside/outside representation usually treat them as outsiders, but I believe they should properly be regarded as insiders.

dent, a dean, or a professor. Larger and more prestigious company boards are likely to include academic representatives from equally prestigious educational institutions.

Board meetings are usually held monthly, except for August, and last anywhere from one to two-and-a-half hours, but quarterly meetings are quite common. The practice in some companies is to follow or precede the meeting with a luncheon to which insiders who are not members of the board are invited. Frequently at the luncheon a company division manager—not necessarily on the board—will make a brief presentation of his divisional operations, describing the product line, method of distribution, product developments, sales, profits, competition, and organizational relationships to other divisions in the company. The purpose of the presentation is to help outside directors learn the operations of the company and get acquainted with the key executives, and, as one president stated, "To build the morale of key divisional people by inviting them to meet informally with the board."

Each position at the board table will have a book, usually leather bound with the director's name embossed in gold, containing the agenda, information and financial results for the period, and memoranda pertinent to the topics to be covered. There are many and varied approaches to the seating of directors, for instance the simple and controversy-avoiding technique of arranging the directors around the table alphabetically starting at the chairman's right, or perhaps assigning the seats closest to the chairman to outside members who have been on the board longest—an arrangement similar to that used in the United States Supreme Court.

After approval by the board of the minutes of the previous meeting, the next item on the agenda is usually a review of operations for the last period—month or quarter. This may be given by the president or the vice president of finance. Divisional or functional managers may report on their respective operations or elaborate on the comments made by their superiors. Depending upon the size and complexity of the company, the financial report will take from thirty minutes to an hour.

This is followed by board approvals of actions of the executive committee taken since the last meeting. The next item is often concerned with capital appropriations requiring board approval—the standard may be that requests for anything over, say, $100,000 or $300,000 are required to come to the board. Brief explanations of the capital appropriations are made by the president or by the interested operating vice president, and a motion for approval is customarily made by one of the outsiders.

A particular agenda might include one or more of the following items:

- Consideration of a refinancing plan.
- Liquidation of obsolete or surplus plants.
- Dividend action.
- Consideration of an acquisition proposed by management.
- Company's position and risks of devaluation abroad.
- A report of research and development programs and products.

During the meeting typically few if any questions are asked by outside directors, and rarely are questions asked by insiders.

After a motion to adjourn is approved, the meeting is over. The old tradition of distributing gold coins as directors' fees at the end of the meeting has been supplanted by prompt post-meeting mailing of checks for the appropriate meeting fee.

There are, of course, many variations of the procedure,

but this description is typical of a monthly or quarterly meeting of a corporate board of directors.

Evidence collected from the field research interviews indicates that three important functions are performed by boards of directors:[3]

1. The board provides advice and counsel.
2. The board serves as some sort of discipline.
3. The board acts in crisis situations.

PROVIDING ADVICE AND COUNSEL

Boards of directors in most companies do serve as a source of advice and counsel to the president. The advisory function of boards was described in a variety of ways by the presidents interviewed.

• Said one president: "The board of directors serves as a sounding board—a wall to bounce the ball against. It is a kind of screen on major moves, whether it be acquisitions, or whether it be major shifts of policy or product line—the broad directions of the business. Board members serve as sources of information. . . . The decision is not made by the board, but the directors are a checkpoint for the management in adding their experience and knowledge to the program."

• Another president said: "If management is capable of taking the advice and using the contacts that a board member can

---

[3] The reader is cautioned to keep in mind that the findings reported in Chapters II and III were derived from corporate situations in which presidents and members of the boards of directors owned only a few shares of stock in the companies served. The effect of substantial stock ownership or the legal representation of stock ownership, such as a trustee of a family trust, on what boards and board members do is discussed in Chapter IV. Also, this report is largely on what outside directors do. The role of inside directors is reported separately in Chapter VI.

provide to them, then that's the best that a board member can bring to them, to the management. Now this obviously requires a board member who can understand the structure of the business, the avenues open to the business for growth, and with some competence to help guide it. The management of a company, after all, has to be turned inward to a considerable extent. They've got to worry about the day-to-day operations. The board can do wonders for the management by providing wisdom from the outside world—windows through which other points of view are added to management thinking, which is a multiplication of the sources of information for better management decisions. I think that all outside directors think that they are advising management, and I think that very few of them think that they are doing anything more. If you ask a hundred or so directors whom I know well what they conceive their function to be, 99½ percent will say, 'To advise the management.' "

• "I think of a board as a sort of cabinet, a group of generalists, not specialists, who can advise me on all kinds of problems, new ideas, new services, improvements on what we are doing, and criticisms of what we are doing. A cabinet is an assemblage of sources of advice—the cabinet name is a good one for a board."

• "Let's just be honest. My board is a group of advisors and they know it. I select and throw up ideas, opportunities, and problems to them and they respond. The board is not a decision-making body. Although there may be times when it could rise up and say no, that is foolhardy. But I hope that we in management are never stupid enough to come up with that kind of a proposal."

• "Boards are not in a position to second-guess our management strategy, but they at least can be sure that we are following a somewhat consistent strategy, and that we are not changing strategy three times a year. They can be helpful by indicating that the management should look into areas they feel management has not carefully explored. They can post words of warning, if you will, to the management, and these are bound to have an effect on management thinking. They can exercise a number of these advisory roles which influence management without actually making decisions or even without management really being sure whether the majority of the board agrees with the recommendation or the advice that has been given by a single board member."

• "I put the directors to work by sending out, prior to the meeting, a rather short and succinct memorandum stating the pro's and con's—why we are doing this, and what the alternatives are. If you do that, you'll find that nearly all the directors will read the stuff, because they are afraid to come to the meeting without having read it. This is a kind of a dirty trick on directors. At the meeting I expect them to comment and make suggestions. Now, they don't have the technical background to say yes or no on a proposal, but they can give advice on the general political situation in a particular country, or maybe on the economic situation—is this the right time to be doing it. They can raise questions and make general suggestions like that. The precise way of describing this role is 'to advise and counsel the management.' "

• A board member said: "The only decision which we as directors will ever make in that company will be to fire the president, and things have to get pretty awful before we would ever do that. All the rest of our job is to advise the management."

• Perhaps the strongest, but not a typical, statement was provided by one president who said: "We get a little advice from the outside board members, but the management runs the company. The board rubber-stamps the action of management, and the board members are there to mollify the outside stockholders."

A few situations were found in which the top management and outside members of the board believed that the role of the board was more than advisory. These were exceptions.

• The chairman of one company stated: "Having been a president and a chief executive officer, I would hate like hell to run a company without a board of directors. I don't know why

I feel this way. It must be that they do serve some purpose. In other words, without a board I would feel as if I were walking around in the cold. You come to the board for recommendations, and you have the comfort of feeling that a group of, you hope, intelligent people have sat down and, with as much time as they have at their disposal, have jointly and individually thought about what you were talking about, and you are glad to have their questions, their challenges, and their approval. Before you get through one of these procedures, I think you have a feeling that the board has served a very valuable purpose. So it is hard for me to say that a board is only advisory. I feel that it is an important part of the corporate structure, and that it does in fact take positions and effectively make decisions."

• The president of another company, speaking as a director, said: "As a director you advise a president, and if he accepts the advice, that's fine. But if he does not take your advice and it's ignored and resented, then I think you have problems. If enough other people on the board feel the same way, then I think you had better do something about it and make a decision. Enough of this lovemaking at the advisory level! But remember, this is some sort of a revolution. If one outside director starts something, he had better have some friends, because if he doesn't, he is dead as a director. I can give you many examples of this. I would not stay on a board as an outside director if my role was regarded by the president only as advisory. I could not be happy if my advice, our advice, was not heeded."

Many examples of the kinds of advice provided by outside directors were given during the interviews, both by presidents as the recipients and users of the advice and by outside directors. The advice and counsel covered a wide area of functions and topics. A few illustrations follow.

Technological Assistance

The impact of technology on almost all companies provides opportunities for directors with technical training and experience to provide advice and counsel to company presidents.

• "I will give you an example of the kind of advice a board member can sometimes give, or at least the kind of question a board member can be in a position to ask, along the lines we have been talking about. The development of satisfactory non-reinforced plastic pipe for very high pressure applications has been an objective of the chemical industry for many years. Many United States companies have been working on the problem, but with limited success. The president of a company which I have served as an outside director was approached to consider participating in a joint venture with a foreign chemical company to develop such a product for the market. Now I knew from personal experience that such a development was no simple business and I wondered whether the state of technology was such as to make such a product economically attractive at that time. I went to some of my friends who had been involved in this field and who had current experience with a similar product. They strongly recommended that we lay off for a year or so since they could not yet see a profitable end to their own venture. The technology was extremely involved and not yet mature. For a company with limited background in a new field, information like this can be quite valuable. I think a good board member should be able to give meaningful advice, or at least ask penetrating questions in some field. I cannot tell them what the interest rate on money is going to be next year; maybe somebody can, but I cannot. But at least in a technical area, where I have some knowledge and contacts, I can bring in advice.

"I don't think that as a director I can tell them to quit working on an idea. About all I can say is, 'Feed these data into the management system that's appraising the rate at which you want to go along and see if maybe it doesn't slow you down by a year or two years.' I do think that is still advisory."

Financial Expertise

The financial expertise in corporate financial staffs obviously varies among companies, regions, and industries—requirements for these skills vary, and the availability of financial skills varies. It was found that for some presidents a knowledgeable, financially oriented outside board member was a source of valuable advice.

• "Several years ago the president of a large insurance company came on our board and began looking over our financial operations. After one of his early board meetings he stopped by my office and observed that our stock was rather low in price, that we had some convertibles that were going to mature, that maybe a good thing to do would be to buy out some of our own stock. We followed his suggestion and saved, I think, over $7 million. If he never does one more thing for this company, he deserves directors' fees for the rest of his life. Clearly he was of enormous help to me, and to our financial people, and the company."

• "I believe that today we in top management need sophisticated financial advice on the board. We cannot maintain these skills internally, and besides, the financial environment is constantly changing. It used to be local, then regional, then national, and now the area for sources of funds is international. In my experience the average top executive—including me—in relation to his role and financial responsibility is technically naïve about the intricacies of finance today. I don't mean just the mechanics of a special deal, but what is the impact of what we are doing on the whole company. I think there has to be outside objective advice on that, because it's not going to come from the company treasurer—he's probably the father of what is being considered."

• "Able outside directors who have the time can contribute to a big publicly held corporation where the corporation has a particular problem, and the director has a skill in that area. Let me illustrate. I am a director of the Acme Construction Company. As you well know, their life-long problem is the availability of capital, because it is a most highly capital-intensive business, and they are highly leveraged. One of the other outside directors is a real financial pro, and I can't tell you how valuable his advice has been. If you had an insurance company man, a commercial banker, or an investment banker, they would all have their particular slant. Here is an outside director without any special bank identification, and he goes across all of them. In this case the company has a financial problem where it needs broad-gauge guidance in its financial policies."

• "I, as a commercial banker, do my dead level best to keep in constant touch with the financial side of the company. The more I know about the inside operations of the company, the better and sounder are my comments and advice to the management. I have lunch periodically with the executive vice president and the vice president of finance, and go over the figures. I review their reports, and the first thing I look at is, what's happened to our receivables, what's happened to our inventory, what's happened to our bank debt. And I tell them outside of meetings, as well as at board meetings, what I think. I make recommendations and suggestions. But it would be a terrible mistake if I ever tried to dictate to the management by putting, for example, a flat debt ceiling on the company. I think we can let management know we think that they have gone too high on their debt, that they have borrowed too damn much money, that the debt position is dangerous—but to sit there and vote a flat ceiling would cause all kinds of problems."

Government Relations

Some presidents with increasing problems of relationships with state and federal government agencies have added former members of government administration offices to their boards. They explained that while it would be inappropriate to ask such a board member to represent the company with a government agency, it was exceedingly helpful to have on the board persons with experience in government who could interpret what goes on in the various agencies and make suggestions for proper approaches to business-government problems.

• "Our business is closely interlocked with Washington regulations," one president said, "and our future is closely tied to the rules and regulations that come out of Washington. We need someone on the board who is a veteran of the Washington scene, who knows and understands the people involved in the executive and legislative branches of the government, and who keeps an eye on what is going on in Washington. Somebody who knows a little bit about the mining business and who has had Washington experience does make a great contribution on our board."

• "Our company is big on technology and government contracts for Research and Development. To have on the board a former Assistant Secretary for Research is terribly valuable, not in participating in specific projects, but helping us evaluate the directions of government-sponsored projects. It would be inappropriate to ask him to call on any agency, but he can and does help by identifying the major opportunity areas for future funding."

• "I think each director who has a specialty should and can be called on in person as an expert on a particular thing. For example, I use Mr. Young on a question of how I approach a problem, say, in Washington at the highest level—let's say in the State Department. I do not trade on whom he knows, but ask, 'How would the State Department operate in such an environment with regard to investment guarantees and that sort of thing?' And if we have a problem with HEW, Mr. Young knows the professional people there from his experiences in Washington, and he can advise where we are most likely to get solutions quickly."

Other Areas of Expertise

Several presidents observed that their outside directors with specialized knowledge and experience in real estate and agriculture have provided valuable inputs to management thinking.

• "It's only relatively recently that we and a lot of other companies began to think of our real estate in the same way we think about our plants of bricks and mortar. One of our recent additions to the board is an oil company executive with responsibilities and experiences in real estate. He is particularly valuable to us as he knows a hell of a lot about real estate locations and how to select them, because of all of their service stations throughout this country. He knows the geography, and raises penetrating and constructive questions which are helpful to me in making decisions on the locations of our new stores. Another thing about advice on real estate. I never realized, before talking with our oil company executive director, how many variations and permutations were possible in the financing of long-term real estate deals."

• "Quite a few of our directors have special and particular areas of competence, and the president, knowing this, will very often talk to them about a proposal on a program before it gets into the form of a memorandum or a recommendation to the board itself on a formal basis. The Webbers, for example, are professionally and personally interested in a number of fields, but especially agriculture. They have substantial holdings here in this country and in Australia."

The surge during the decade of the 1960s in achieving corporate growth through the acquisition of other enterprises was another area of advice and counsel identified by those interviewed.

• "When I went on the Benson Publishing Company board it was for the agreed-upon purpose of advising them as they embarked on a program of diversification. My company had a fine reputation for growing soundly through planned acquisitions, and the publishing business represented no conflict with my own product lines. I helped them initiate a plan for growth, advised on the organization of the staff, and guided them as they accomplished what I think was an enormously successful effort."

• "One of my outside directors is a real pro on acquisitions, and he has been most helpful to me. He does not know much about our operations or our problems, but he does know a lot about the process of identifying and acquiring other companies. Also he knows the people involved, and this is useful. There is a lot of stuff on acquisitions that is common in all acquisitions. He has been through a bundle of them and has helped me through some rough spots—in negotiating, for example."

Another area in which it was found that outside directors were helpful to presidents was company pension plans and executive compensation plans, including options and bonuses.

• "On pension-plan management nobody can say for sure what's right and what's wrong. Most top executives are concerned about the problem, and it can be useful to get the experiences of a number of outside directors who are also presidents of big companies. These kinds of problems are in a sense nonoperating; they are not unique to any one company or industry. They are the general problems that every company has. And when some outside director says, 'Well, here is what we did, and here are the results after we did it,' something worthwhile is added."

• "Will Wright, who is president of a very large company, is on our board, and he does not know a lot about the telecommunications business, but he has been particularly helpful to me in the area of pension-fund management. Every company that has trusteed pension funds runs into the same set of problems, where you are not entirely satisfied with the performance of one or more trustees. An interchange of information on what you do about the set of conditions is valuable, and it's far more helpful to hear from Will Wright than it would be from some trust officer of a bank. It is a different, but a terribly important, point of view."

SERVING AS SOME SORT OF DISCIPLINE

In addition to providing a resource for advice and counsel, it was found that boards of directors serve as some sort of discipline for company presidents and subordinate managements. The company president and his associates know that at least once a month, or once a quarter, they are required to appear before the board of directors and account for the operations of the enterprise. While the president is reasonably sure that the outside directors will not raise any embarrassing questions, the very requirement of appearing before his directors, who are usually respected peers in the business world, is a discipline itself not only for the president but also for the insiders on the board and insiders who are not on the board. The latent possibility that questions might be asked requires that the top executives of the company analyze their present situation and be prepared to answer all possible questions which might—but probably will not—be raised by friendly directors.

• One president described the discipline value of an outside board as follows: "Just as I conduct a performance review every month of each of our divisions, I think it is essential for the board to be the instrument before which we have a performance review of the company as a whole. To that extent, just as I don't make operating decisions for a division, so the board does not make operating decisions for me. Nevertheless, there is an essential discipline in having to appear at the board meeting with a distillate of the relevant facts and figures of the company, an analysis of the problems, and most particularly a program as to what we are going to do about the problems. This discipline of course reflects itself all the way down through the organization, because knowing that we have a board meeting coming up, the operating division heads have to be prepared to discuss their problems and their solutions with me. Our key executives are members of the board, and while we may not get into their problems in depth at the board meeting, they are sure that if they come up as major problems, they had better be prepared to comment on the problems in the presence of all the directors. This is an excellent discipline in that the division managers are required on a monthly basis to analyze their operations, identify problems, formulate solutions, and be held accountable for the results. Representations on solutions to identify division problems constitute a commitment for action."

• Another president stated: "The fact that you know that outsiders are going to be looking at what you have done, and what you are doing, forces you into doing a little better job. There is a discipline factor here. We go to a lot of trouble to make sure that what we present to the board is well thought through, and an attractively presented proposal—we want to manifest that the proposal is a product of thoughtful management. I am sure that if we did not have to account periodically to the board we would become a lot more casual and informal in our operations. I don't know whether this reaction is fact or fiction. But I think we behave differently internally, knowing that we have outside directors. The mere existence of outside directors makes us think a little bit harder, makes us organize our thoughts. It sharpens up the whole organization."

• "A board in my opinion is a very good discipline for a management, and one which the management may wish to impose on itself. The very fact that you report on a fairly formal basis once every month—which is our practice—makes you give that little extra effort. Sure, you can go and hire a consultant. You can go to Washington and get a guy. But maybe we don't do these things as religiously as if once a month you report to a group who, in the final analysis, do represent the owners, the stockholders—even though we can argue about the fiction of stockholder representation by the board.

"Also this discipline thing is good for the organization. The chairman and I don't do all the reporting. In fact we do very little of it. We bring into the board meetings eight or ten inside men who are not members of the board. They are often there for the full meeting, and the only time they'll get excused is towards the end when such matters as officers' salaries or something like that come up. The outside board members get to know who is around the place in addition to the chairman and the president. It's good training for the individuals within the company to make ten or fifteen minute reports to the board on their respective operations. Good training, and good discipline."

• "If a company did not have a board of outside directors, it might be a little bit more free-wheeling, a little bit more careless, and a little bit more lax than it would otherwise be. Knowing that they must appear before, in a sense, their professional peers, and report on what they in management have done, is a healthy thing for management."

• "It goes back to where I describe the only role of a board. If top management and the few people at the top wish to use the board, they can increase profits by making people down the organizational lines think. This is using the board as a disciplinary thing. Boards can't make people think, but management uses the board as a means to make people think. I use the technique all the time. This morning, for example, I had a staff meeting. I said, 'What the hell. If we don't do it this way, supposing some member of the board should ask me a question about this damn thing. Who in the hell around here is going to answer?' These are just the words I used at the meeting this morning. This is a sort of a Machiavellian approach, but you know the Prince was not too unwise.

"Let me give you another example. About fifteen years ago we acquired a family business owned by two brothers. They had male children down below, and they all got into the act when decisions had to be made. This was a fairly substantial business. We paid over $35 million for the whole show. All of the decisions which they had made were sort of made in the family conclave—nothing in writing, nothing formal, no estimates, no outcome figures. It was all done by intuitive feeling, seat-of-the-pants, or whatever you want to call it. We got hold of one of the sons, who was a pretty bright guy. He had been in the company ever since he graduated from the Harvard Law School. We made him chief executive officer of the subsidiary, and told him about the formality of a board of directors—

that authorization for expenditures all had to be done in advance, and all that kind of stuff. I thought he would be very upset about it because of all the bureaucratic paper work. But I did not suggest the procedures: I imposed them upon him, as the rules of the road. After about a year or so I went by and said, 'How do you like our system?' And to my surprise he said, 'I think it's just great—it's great because it makes us think things out.'

"Here was the reaction of a fellow who had been brought up in a family company without any board worth talking about, and yet he welcomed complying with the discipline of outside board members. So again I say, a board of directors can be used by management to impose discipline on the staff, to do things up right, to submit thoughtful proposals in writing, and so forth."

• "In the last three years we have changed from a management board of directors to a board where the outsiders outnumber the management members. And I can tell you very frankly that this change has caused all of us in management to prepare ourselves better than we ever did before. It's been a good thing for our own people, because they had to do their homework more professionally; and as a by-product I think it's resulted in our getting better people on the staff."

Many top executives, in describing the discipline role of boards of directors, used the phrase "corporate conscience."

• Typical of the comments was: "The board is, in a very real sense, a corporate conscience that the management is aware that they should go to, have to go to, for approval. If management did not have this requirement, I wonder what the ceiling or limits would be on what management might do. The conscience role of the board is a device that makes sure that homework is being done, and that criteria are thought through and proposed. The conscience function is involved in capital appropriations, operating budgets, compensation decisions, and others. The board is not really a decision-making body, but it is involved in the decision-making process as a sort of corporate conscience. The board rarely, if ever, rejects out of hand a

proposal by the president, but their existence in the management scheme of things influences the president and helps keep
his decisions within the bounds of conscionable conduct."

• Another president observed: "On company compensation
policies and administration, I think the outside directors on a
compensation committee do serve as a conscience. In our case,
when the personnel vice president and I prepare recommendations on salary changes that are to be reviewed with three outside directors, I think there is a tendency to do a more objective
job. It doesn't go much beyond the conscience role, though,
because if the outside directors tend to interfere, they dilute
my responsibilities and authority. I've got to live with, and get
results out of, the organization on a day-to-day basis; the outside board members on the compensation committee do not
have to."

ACTING IN CRISIS SITUATIONS

In addition to serving as a source of advice and counsel,
and as some sort of discipline for company managements,
boards of directors, it was found, do fulfill a critically important function when confronted with crisis situations.
With their ultimate legal responsibility for the corporation, boards take active decision-making roles (1) when the
president dies unexpectedly and a replacement must be
designated; and (2) when the management performance
becomes so unsatisfactory that a change in the office of the
president must be made.

When a 45-year-old president dies suddenly or becomes
incapacitated—a not uncommon occurrence in today's competitive world—the board of directors has a decision-making
responsibility to select and elect his successor. In some
situations it was found that the selection process was aided
and in effect largely controlled by the deceased president,
who had taken the precaution of discussing with board

members what he wanted them to do "if he was hit by a truck one day." In other cases, with no evidence that the president's health was vulnerable, board members and presidents alike neglected doing much about the problem of succession. It was only when confronted with the unexpected death of a president that boards were suddenly propelled into a decision-making function. But the board was there—legally constituted to pick a successor, and to ensure the continuity of an entity organized to operate in perpetuity. The de facto powers of control dropped by the deceased president were then picked up and exercised by the board: "The king is dead, long live the king."

The second crisis situation, and one which is much more difficult for the board to face and cope with, is when the profitability of the enterprise declines steadily, and increasing evidence suggests that the principal problem is the capacity of the president to manage the enterprise successfully and profitably. It is then, as one president stated, that "the board of directors becomes the center of authority, and must become active and effective in the case of almost disaster."

• The importance of the board's role under these conditions was described by one president. "In my opinion the most important and key function of the board is to decide whether management is doing a good job, and then face that difficult question: 'Do we change management, or don't we?' When everything is going well, I don't think it makes a great deal of difference who sits on the board. When things go badly, when it's necessary to make fundamental changes in the management of the company, at this point I think the board exercises its maximum effectiveness—really, its key effectiveness. When the board is monitoring the management, it is watching what is going on. As long as it is happy with what's going on, whether the members ask abrasive questions or whether they don't ask abrasive questions is really unimportant. But if the company starts faltering, and it becomes obvious for one reason or another that the company doesn't have proper management, a group of outsiders needs to make the key decision—whether to change the management."

• Another top executive said: "So long as the management is doing all right there is no reason for the board to do anything except to be in a position to make a decision if something really goes wrong. But most boards don't evaluate the president until things go to hell. If the situation starts to decline, earnings are going down, and there is no program to arrest that trend, then the outside directors start to evaluate management. They ask, 'What is the management's program? And I want to know whether that program is going to arrest the decline, because I see disaster ahead if it isn't arrested.' "

• "There are a reasonable number of directors," said the executive vice president of a New York based company, "who meet the test of trying to push managements into thinking about their business. But there are very few directors whom I have seen who ever take any effective action in the area of being sure that the quality of management is up to standard, or up to what it should be. To suggest to management that you as an outside director think the management is incompetent is done only when things get very, very tough. And even then the board members I know are not going to do anything, regardless of how they feel, except resign at the earliest propitious moment."

Measuring management, and fulfilling the key function of deciding whether management is doing a good job, and facing the difficult question "Does management have to be changed?" is a most difficult task for any outside director.

• The response of one president to the question, "How is the performance of a president measured by the board?" was: "I don't really know. I think the phrase is a bunch of jargon. How in the world can any outside board member know whether I'm doing a good job? They don't know the problems, and they have no way of deciding whether I do a good job of solving them or not."

• "I have neither seen nor heard of any boards that do an effective job of score-keeping on the performance of management. And this is not really surprising. Outside board members really don't know whether or not you are running, say, your manufacturing operations well or poorly. How do they know if we have obsolete equipment in half our plants? How do they know whether we are maintaining our facilities or deferring maintenance costs to protect this year's profits? They don't. These typically are the kinds of things that have a slow and, over a period of time, definite effect on earnings.

"Also, how can you as an outside director calibrate how good the management of my company is this year? We're not having a good year. The bad part of our business is in residential housing. Sure, housing starts are off. Money is tight. And there has been an enormous increase in the manufacture and sale of mobile homes. Maybe we should have recognized the profit opportunities in mobile homes and shifted our resources to take advantage of that relatively new and booming approach to shelter. How can an outside director come to any real conclusion that we ought to be replaced?—He can't."

• This viewpoint was confirmed by a president who said: "It seems to me that a board is handicapped in exercising the responsibility to measure management unless it has more than a casual amount of time to spend on the company's business. To exercise that function, a board member has got to work at it, and I think the man who serves on several boards and has a fulltime job some place else just can't do it. He is not sufficiently knowledgeable, he is not sufficiently concerned, and he doesn't have the time to do it."

Another difficulty in measuring management is that the outside board members can respond only or principally to the material and data which are presented. It should be noted here that appraising the president's performance can be limited by what the president, who controls the sources of information, chooses to make available.

• Commenting on this point, the president of a large eastern company said: "It's pretty easy for a smart management to snow a board of directors right up to the time that the profits start to cave in, and by that time it's too damn late to do anything. The board has so little access to inside information of a company. The board can tell whether the company is at work in a growing field, whether its image in the country is good or bad, whether the management makes a good personal impression and seems alert and answers questions reasonably well. But I don't see how a board can tell whether a company has marketing practices that in a period of two or three years are going to start losing ground to a more aggressive competitor, or whether a company has processes and manufacturing plant which are likely to be outmoded by some competitor in the next five years. It's just difficult for issues of basic importance to a company's economic operation to be available to the board, unless the chief executive officer recognizes that the board members can give him some help, and is willing to throw the bad and the good on the table for them."

• "It's a perfectly natural human reaction to hold back on your problems when confronted by an intelligent bunch of directors. No board members can help you on something you're successfully in already. You don't need any help. That's what boards are likely to hear about. A guy running a company is afraid that if he throws out the problems as well as the successes, it will make him look less successful."

• "When I first went on the board of the Rawson Company as a division manager, our division sales were over $200 million. I used to prepare a report, which I presented to the board, and I talked about progress, accomplishments against plan, and then I said, 'Here are my problems.' After several months people got tired of hearing about my problems, so I never did that any more. I guess the outside directors began to feel that if I couldn't handle the problems without involvement by the board, the division probably needed a new manager."

• Another example of the difficulty a board has in evaluating the performance of the president was found in the Barnes Company. During the 1950s and early 1960s the Barnes Company was the leader in the industry it served. Sales and profits increased impressively, and the outside board members enjoyed the prestige of the company identification, but knew relatively little about the company's condition or about what was happening in the industry.

In the middle 1960s electronic developments in the industry began to encroach on the company's market share and market position. The president, aged 60, who had headed the company for fifteen years, refused to recognize the threat of technological developments. In fact he refused internal suggestions to add electronic engineers to the company's research and development organization. Over a four-year period the company sales plummeted, and profits disappeared. In 1968 the company was acquired by an English company seeking a foothold in the United States market.

An outside director of the Barnes Company, reflecting on the company's decline, said, "We outsiders on the board got all of our information on the threat of technological change through the president. He didn't see, or refused to see, what was going on, and we on the board just sat there listening to the siren song of that gracious, articulate Southerner who was president."

When conditions in a company deteriorate because of what seems to be the incompetence of the president, and the outside directors become uneasily aware that some action needs to be taken by the board, three alternative courses were found to be employed.

(1) *Hire a management consultant.* Employing management consultants to recommend the taking of unpleasant management actions is not an uncommon approach to difficult and sensitive problem areas. Certainly one of these is the problem of a group of friendly outside board members trying to communicate to a company president that he is not doing a satisfactory job as chief executive officer. Periodic total management and organization audits by competent professional consultants are performed for very successful company managements who are aware that corporate suc-

cess may be dulling their responses to change. Accordingly the suggestion by a group of outside directors that consultants be employed to review a company's operations is consistent with good management practice, and therefore not immediately offensive to the president.

• The executive vice president of a large eastern company described a recent experience. "I and a few other outside directors of a very substantial company in the United States were quite unhappy about the management. They seemed not to be doing what they talked about with regard to product line change. Our difficulty at the board level was especially tough because the company's earnings were fairly good. The management just didn't seem to be doing anything differently from five years ago, ten years ago, and fifteen years ago. They had no plans for looking to the future. They never talked about the future. They were unconcerned about competition, and did not care about what could or might happen to the business.

"I chatted with the president after a board meeting and told him that I had a good many acquaintances among the major management consulting firms in New York; that in the eastern company where I am a director one consulting firm had been most helpful in developing a corporate planning function; and that it might be worthwhile to check with a consultant to determine what if anything they might do for us. The president was responsive, and arrangements were made for a management audit. Here is the surprising result. A recommendation by the consultants that the president move up to a position as chairman of the board and that a younger outside executive be employed as president was accepted by the president—and of course by the board."

(2) *Resign from the board.* Resignation from the board was found to be the most common and typical response of a director who has concluded that the company's president is inadequate.

• One president said: "I resigned from the Fox board because the chief executive officer, who was an old friend, had assembled a group of mediocre executives who just weren't going to take the company anywhere. I concluded that I didn't have a ghost of a chance to effectuate changes internally—that if I tried, it would be resisted. So I simply resigned. Now I recognize that an argument can be made that you have a duty to shareholders to do something about it. But I think I fulfilled that responsibility when I tried to do what can be done within the structure. Having failed to operate effectively within the structure, I didn't want to be engaged in undermining the management. I admit there is a logical inconsistency, because if you are elected to represent the shareholders, maybe you should do it to the last extreme. But I think that in the world in which we live, life is just too short. I view my main business role in life to be the operation of the company where I am president. I wouldn't want to get involved in a full-time or major time-consuming activity on behalf of somebody else."

• "About five years ago a friend of mine became president of a medium-sized company on the west coast, and shortly after becoming president he asked me to go on the board. He had carte blanche authority to restructure the board, and he decided to ask all the old-time insiders to withdraw from the board so that the board would consist of the president and six new out-side directors. I accepted the board membership, and found myself in the company of some very distinguished names from that region's business world.

"During the next three years the president and his corporate planning staff were very active in identifying and recommending the acquisition of eight or ten relatively small companies that appeared to have some product line and common technology relationship. The acquisition program seemed to make sense, and the board approved each one recommended. But then the monthly financial reports began to indicate that the forecasted earnings of the newly acquired companies were not being realized, and that the earnings of the company's traditional business were declining. About this time the president scheduled a two-day board meeting in San Francisco, so that the board members could visit the plants of the recently acquired companies, and attend a board meeting the following day.

"We visited the headquarters and plants of five subsidiaries, and it became completely clear to me that the technological relationship among the acquisitions was remote and not real, that none of the acquisitions had much promise, and that the president and the board probably had made some very wrong decisions in taking on these small enterprises.

"At dinner that night I talked to the president about my conclusions, and he disagreed violently. He was adamant in defending the acquisition decisions and the operations of the subsidiaries. I was convinced that errors of judgment had been made by the president, so when I returned home I wrote him a three-page letter outlining my reasons for resigning. I was sure he was on the wrong track and that he could not be persuaded to change his course. I could have stayed on and watched the company turn in even worse financial results—as it did. But that's not much fun either. I chose not to be identified with a president and a company where I was sure greater problems were ahead, so I resigned. When brokers and investment bankers called asking the reason for my resignation, I told them that there was a product-line conflict with another company where I was a director, and that I had to resign from one or the other."

• "Your alternative is to get off the board. Because if you are not satisfied with the conduct of the business, and you conclude you just can't assist, aid, or influence its course of action, then if you are a so-called professional type outside director, you resign. Now if you own 5 percent or 10 percent of the stock, or you represent some foundation with substantial holdings, you've got to stay on even though you don't like what is going on. And then you're going to be a real miserable son-of-a-bitch as far as the rest of the directors are concerned. But if you are just a garden-variety outside director and you become disenchanted with the president, you avoid conflict by resigning. Conflict, you know, does no good.

"You can say that resignation is closing your eyes to the

problem, but this is not entirely so. The stockholders' interest may be served indirectly by your resignation. If a couple of outside people with some prominence depart from the board of a company, it is not going to do the company any great good in the eyes of the investment community, the commercial banking community, and all those guys. This starts putting a question mark around the company itself. There again, I think most managements with much brains just don't have directors leave for no good reason. You start getting write-ups in the financial magazines, a *Wall Street Journal* reporter calls, and it's just not good. The first thing you know a New York bank asks, 'What's the problem here?' And maybe you owe them 10 million bucks. You've got lines of credit. This is bad. People who aren't smart enough to know all these things don't usually get to be chief executives of companies anyway."

Directors who resign because of lack of confidence in the president usually find some plausible and acceptable rationale which does not result in the questions cited by the director quoted above. The increasing pressure of one's own company's requirements; the desire to take it a little easier at age 60; health reasons—the executive's or his wife's; the interest of the United States Justice Department in product-line conflicts or interlocking directorates—all serve the purpose of the resigning director as well as the company from which he is resigning.

(3) *Take action requesting the president to resign.* Occasionally a financial page of the press carries a brief story: "It was announced today by Mr. R. J. Jones, Chairman of the XYZ Company, that Mr. Paul Brown, president, resigned because of policy differences with the board." In companies where management and outside directors own little common stock, it is rare that outside directors take the drastic action outlined in the press release of asking the president to resign. If the president is involved in a personal scandal such as the commission of a major crime or in

conflicts of interest from which he has profited personally at the company's expense, or if he is identified with bribery or some other generally unacceptable conduct, the resignation of the president is not uncommon. But when the president is *not* guilty of any of these transgressions, and his only shortcoming is the lack of capacity to manage the company effectively, then outside directors are most reluctant to ask for his resignation. Reasons for the directors' reluctance are discussed in Chapter V.

Asking a president to resign is a traumatic experience under any circumstances. Loyalties, working relationships, and social relationships all get in the way of complete objectivity in appraising and concluding what is best for the company. Most outside directors try to avoid the high level of emotion that almost always attends a forced resignation. As indicated earlier, most outside directors resign to avoid the unpleasantness inevitably involved. And even some of those who choose not to resign, but to stay and participate in an eventual solution, tend to procrastinate and to defer the ultimate but necessary decision. They seem to keep hoping that things will somehow improve. This attitude was found particularly in outside directors who had professional financial or legal-service relationships with the company.

• In one case poor management by the president resulted in the steady decline of sales and profits in a once-profitable and distinguished midwestern company. There were seven outside board members on a board of sixteen, and although there was mounting evidence that the president was incapable of leading the enterprise, no action was initiated by the board members. Finally, after a succession of three loss years, a vice president of the principal lending bank, and not a director of the company, asked to meet with the board, and stated that unless a change was made, the bank loans would not be renewed. With this leverage from the bank, the outside directors made the decision to ask the president to resign—but, it should be noted, with considerable reluctance.

• In another company with fifteen board members, eight of whom were insiders, earnings had declined steadily for eighteen months. Concerned about the company's leadership, the seven outside directors met to discuss what, if anything, should be done. Most of the directors reluctantly concluded that the president had to be terminated, but two directors pleaded for other solutions. They suggested that the president be promoted to a post to be created for the occasion—vice chairman of the board. Or that the president be named chairman of the finance committee. Or that he keep the title as president and the vice president be asked to take over as chief executive officer.[1] These suggested compromises were rejected by the other five outside directors, and the president was forced to resign.

• The president of another company recounted an experience of a fellow director. "A responsible board member on the board *can* be there when it counts. One of my closest friends, Dave Donald, a partner of an investment banking firm, was a director of the Paine Company. You remember the to-do in the press about this company a year ago. The Paine Company was going down hill rapidly. Bad performance was followed by unbelievably terrible performance. Poor Dave was staying awake nights wondering what to do. If the company went bankrupt, there would be mud on Dave's face. If he resigned, that would be backing away from a deal for which he felt some responsibility. So Dave decided that the only hope for the enterprise was to fire the president. Dave called a couple of other outside direc-

---

[1] Those who have read *The Peter Principle* will recognize instantly that this attempted maneuver would be a perfect example of "percussive sublimation"—an apparent promotion, apparent to outsiders but not to hierarcheologists. Note the difference between "percussive sublimation" and "lateral arabesque." The lateral arabesque is not an apparent promotion but a sideways move out of the stream of operations. When you are dealing with presidents, it is rare that the lateral arabesque can be used. More often the percussive sublimation—the apparent promotion—is the principal and practical alternative. (Laurence J. Peter and Raymond Hull, *The Peter Principle*, New York, William Morrow & Co., 1969.)

tors, and this small group, led by Dave, finally, after some time had passed, was able to get the president to resign. Then, as a search committee, they found an outsider to come in and pick up the pieces. For better or worse—we don't really know yet—a change was made in the presidency. But Dave took it upon himself to fulfill his personal understanding of his responsibilities as a director. It was a huge pain in the neck, but he did it. Here the system worked. Here a director was faced with a problem, and he did not back away. When a company gets to the brink of disaster because of lousy management, who can do anything about it except a director? The old president of Paine certainly was not going to fire himself."

• The president of another company said: "When I came to this company from running my own show in the midwest, the enterprise had gone downhill for three years, and it took the directors too long, in my opinion, to see what was going on. When they finally woke up, a lot of unnecessary damage had been done—bank relationships, labor problems, key people leaving, and so on. But the board liked the old president—he went to Yale, had been a Bones man, and all that stuff. And the company drifted for three years before someone on the board dredged deep into the barrel and got hold of me."

Conclusions

In companies where the president and members of the board of directors own only a few shares of stock, it was found that most boards do provide a source of advice and counsel to the president. Those interviewed—company presidents as well as outside directors—perceived the role of outside directors to be largely advisory and not decision making. Depending upon the abilities, skills, and experiences represented on the board, and the needs of the company managements, advice and counsel were provided in functional areas such as finance, marketing, labor relations, and so on, and in a wide gamut of other subjects—technology, real estate, pension-plan management, acquisitions, and government relations. The inputs of outside directors were valued by top managements, who had generally regarded the board members as "additional windows to the outside world." Outside directors, members of a peer group with the president, typically were accustomed to dealing with business problems of considerable magnitude, and were able to bring a worthwhile point of view to such issues as were presented to the board by the president.

Also it was found that in most companies the boards of directors serve as some sort of discipline for the management—the president as well as those in subordinate positions. Company presidents and their associates know that periodically they are required to appear before the board of directors and to account for their stewardship of the company's operations since the last reporting date. Even though the president is usually quite sure that board members will not ask discerning or penetrating questions, the requirement of a periodic appearance before a board of professional peers does cause the executives to review their operating results, to identify problems, and to give explanations.

Almost all the executives interviewed stated that the concept of accountability to a board, even boards composed of the most understanding and sympathetic friends, provided an important discipline for the organization— "especially the vice presidents," as one executive stated. The feeling of accountability to a legally constituted body such as the board of directors resulted in a closer examination and analysis of results, a more faithful fulfillment of what was called "corporate homework," and an increased interest in avoiding careless and ill-prepared presentations to the board. Boards of directors do provide some sort of discipline for business organizations—a sort of corporate conscience.

It was found also that most boards of directors exercise a decision-making power only in the event of a crisis such as the sudden death or disability of the president, or recognition by the board that the management performance is so unsatisfactory that a change must be made in the presidency.

If the president dies unexpectedly, the board of directors is the legal vehicle in place to assure the continuity of the company's management. Organized to operate in perpetuity, the business corporation is maintained as a going concern by a decision of the board designating a successor.

The other crisis situation where boards of directors fulfill a decision-making role is where the profitability of the enterprise declines steadily, and mounting and persuasive evidence suggests to the board that the president must be replaced as chief executive officer. Several of those interviewed described this role of the board as the only real decision-making job the board has—"The rest is all fluff."

It was found that boards of directors of most companies do not do an effective job in evaluating, appraising, and measuring the company president until the financial and other results are so dismal that some remedial action is forced upon the board. Any board has a difficult job in measuring the performance of a president. Criteria are rarely defined for his evaluation. The president's instinct is to attribute poor results to factors over which he has no control. The inclination of friendly directors is to go along with these apparently plausible explanations. Control of the data made available to the board which provides a basis for evaluation of the president is in the president's own hands, and board members rarely have sufficient interest and time to really understand the critical elements in the operations of the company. Only when the company's results deteriorate almost to a fatal point does the board step in and face the unpleasant task of asking the president to resign.

In those situations where boards of directors conclude

that the president is inadequate in the top executive job, three principal alternatives were found to be used: (1) hire a management consultant to perform an overall management audit; (2) resign from the board for one of many plausible reasons which embarrasses neither the director nor the company; (3) ask the president to resign.

Action by a board to replace the president is a most difficult and emotion-laden management decision, and it was found that this is usually done only when the results of bad performance are overwhelming. Boards of directors of business organizations are reluctant to conclude that the management is not satisfactory.

CHAPTER III

Generally Accepted Roles

To measure what boards of directors actually do against the classical and standard definitions of their functions, I collected evidence during my interviews on three of the generally accepted roles of boards of directors: (1) to establish the basic objectives, corporate strategies, and broad policies of the company; (2) to ask discerning questions; and (3) to select the president.

ESTABLISHING THE BASIC OBJECTIVES, CORPORATE STRATEGIES, AND BROAD POLICIES OF THE CORPORATION

The basic objectives, corporate strategies, and broad policies of companies are not established by the board in most large and medium-sized companies.

- "Management," as one senior executive vice president said, "creates the policies. We decide what course we are going to paddle our canoe in. We tell our directors the direction of the company and the reasons for it. Theoretically the board has a right of veto, but they never exercise it. Naturally we consult with them if we are making a major change in direction. We communicate with them. But they are in no position to challenge what we propose to do."
- A senior partner of a well-known consulting group stated, "I don't know of a single board that I've ever heard of that really digs into the strategy of the business, or sets targets for growth and holds management accountable for the results."

Capital Allocations

To illustrate, a major determinant in the implementation of corporate strategy is the allocation of capital to existing or new areas of operations. It was found that procedures for capital appropriations vary widely. In a few companies the capital budgets or specific capital appropriations are never presented to the board for their information or approval. In most companies, however, the allocation of capital is regarded as an appropriate board matter, although here again procedures vary among companies. In some a proposed capital budget for the following year is presented with considerable detail, and when approved by the board becomes the spending charter for the period. In others an annual capital budget is presented to the board for approval, but any actual expenditure over, say, $100,000 or $300,000 requires a new approval at a board meeting. In some of these companies the capital appropriation request consists of one or two pages highlighting the purpose, the amount requested, the payout, and pro forma figures of the effect on sales and profits. In other companies 40- to 50-page memoranda justify each request for capital. Frequently the same study which is prepared by someone in management in seeking approval from the president is reproduced and distributed to the board members—sometimes before, but usually at, the meeting.

In those few companies where capital allocations are not regarded by management as proper matters for board consideration, the explanations by the company presidents were similar.

• One president stated it succinctly: "I would never take a capital appropriation request to the board. What in the world would they know about it!"

• Another president said: "There is absolutely no point in

asking a board of directors for approval of capital expenditures. It would be a waste of their time and mine. What contribution could any outside director make? Ours is a complex business with national and international implications. To succeed in this industry we have to have within the organization every skill and ability relevant to the kinds of problems we face. We do not look to the board for these skills, because we need them on a continuing and daily basis. For example, if we have studied the merits of investing $5 million or $20 million in a new facility in England, what purpose is served by coming to the board and asking its approval? For any outside director to have the slightest basis for comment, he would have to devote at least a week, and probably more, to full-time study of the working papers. The typical outside director does not have the time to do this. And even if he did, what could he add, really, to the thinking of the specialized experts who made the project study?

"Let me tell you about something that came up recently. Two months ago we introduced a new consumer item and began marketing it on a regional basis. Its acceptance was much greater than we anticipated, and the division manager asked for approval to buy an additional $1 million worth of machinery and equipment to speed up the program for going national. Should we wait two or three weeks for our next board meeting? Certainly not. I did not even bother to call a meeting of the three-man inside executive committee. With the recommendation of the division manager, supported by the market results, I told him to go ahead now, not three weeks from now."

The managements of most companies studied, however, believe that all requests for the allocation of capital resources should be presented to the board of directors for approval. As indicated earlier, the form of the presentation to the board varies.

• In one company the president, in reviewing a batch of selected capital requests, stated: "We show everything to the board over and above $300,000. In the past we have given them a very substantial amount of material on each case. We decided a couple of weeks ago that this was probably more than was needed, so now we're going to present 2 to 3 pages on the small ones, and 20 to 30 pages on the larger requests. In the past we presented hundreds of pages on a given large project. What we did was to bind together the copies of the key working papers. The board can't say we held back on data!"

Whether the management requests for capital appropriations are presented in long form or short form, it was found that in most companies boards of directors do not disapprove of management's recommendations.

• One president said: "Silence by board members is a great disguise. But just from listening to directors over many years, watching how they behave, and calibrating the knowledge they appear to show, I would say that directors tend to read the capital appropriation requests in which they have some experience or some interest, and they pay very little attention to all the rest—they just thumb through them, look at the front page so they know what is being talked about. We have a couple of directors interested in real estate, and when we propose to buy land in Germany for $450,000 there may be a question or two but never, ever, disapproval. In my over twenty years with this company the board has never turned down a request for the appropriation of capital, nor has it ever really seriously challenged our recommendations."

• Another president said: "The board is in no position, and doesn't undertake to be in a position, to challenge or question the specific capital appropriation recommendations of management."

• Another chairman said: "In the seventeen years I've been with this company, and my previous associations, I haven't been turned down by the board yet, that I can consciously remember. If I was, it was on some inconsequential thing, nothing important. The board is not in a particularly good position to say no to management. They don't know the industry. My operations people do. And if they come in and say we ought to expand a particular plant from 2000 tons to 5000 tons a month, how can any outside director say no? Nine hundred and ninety-nine times out of a thousand, the board goes along with management, and our batting average on making the right management decisions is not that good."

Decisions on Company Policies

During the research interviews, chairmen, presidents, and directors were asked if the board was a decision-making body on company policies, strategies, and objectives.

• One chairman said: "I don't think the board can exercise decision making except in a very limited scope. I think the board *can* exercise its decision making in the selection of a chief executive officer and the organization of the very top structure of the company—that is, they can decide whether there should be a president's office or not. They can make decisions as to whether the chief executive officer should or should not be a participant in the company's executive bonus plan. They can make a stop or go decision, if you will, on the amount of capital expenditures in a given period of time." In answer to the question, "But rarely do they go contrary to management?" he said: "Rarely *should* they go contrary to management. But they can be helpful in a number of advisory roles which influence management without actually making decisions."

• A senior executive vice president, an outside director of several companies, said: "The only time the board of directors becomes a decision-making body is when it is dissatisfied with management. When I reach the point of being dissatisfied with management, I don't mind making the decision, and I think that is proper." He continued: "You must remember, the board does not make policies—management makes the policies. I can't think of a single time when the board has failed to support a proposed policy of management or failed to endorse the recommendation of management. If I were president and the three executive vice presidents and I thought a given course was the way to go, whether a diversification move, an acquisition, or what have you, that's the way the company goes. The board will be consulted, but the board does not, can not, make the decision."

• The vice chairman of a large eastern company stated: "Except for the selection of the chief executive officer, the board is basically a nondecision-making body."

• A 55-year-old company vice president who serves as outside director for three corporations said: "With regard to this acquisition kick that everybody seems to be on, I have been involved in at least four or five situations where I learned about a major acquisition by one of my companies when I read it in the paper. Yet those decisions by management determine the strategy of the company for years to come. Also I don't know of any board member who has taken his responsibilities seriously enough to have really looked at the industry, tried to see what was happening, and then got his company management involved in adapting a corporate strategy to the perceived changes. A good example is the meat-packing industry. A revolution has been going on there, pioneered not by the old-established companies but by relative newcomers. Where in the world have the directors of the old line companies been? Of course it's not only meat packing. I could name a dozen other industries. The point is that one of the most important single functions of an outside board member *ought* to be his awareness of other forces at work in the industry in which the company is operating. I don't know of any outside director who fulfills this role."

The conclusion that boards of directors do not create basic objectives, corporate strategy, and broad policies in most companies should be qualified by the evidence found in a few situations. These cases are not typical of those studied, but they do illustrate the role that boards can perform in creating objectives, strategies, and policies.

• The president of a large midwestern cereal manufacturing corporation, the Wehr Company, described his perception of the board as a policy-making body. "I think that what our board does is pretty much what it ought to do. Acting in their primary role as a board, they provide a forum and exercise a collective judgment concerning where the business is going and what the specific solutions to specific problems ought to be. In a sense they exercise judgment, based not only on their knowledge of the company but also on the distillate of the knowledge they have acquired through other connections. We have outside board members with widely diverse backgrounds, and as a group they are in a position to exercise judgment and to make decisions. Now, obviously they don't get involved in a decision-making role on a matter of operating policy. For example, they would not be concerned with an operating decision to spend 4.8 percent of sales on advertising rather than 4.5 percent. But I know they would exercise a decision-making role if, for example, I proposed getting into a new line of business which they felt was not applicable or appropriate to our corporate strategy. Then they would make the decision that the management's recommendation should be overturned. Any president who feels that the board is not a decision-making body in determining corporate strategy doesn't really need a board except to fill some name slots in the annual report."

An outside director of the Wehr Company confirmed the validity of the president's views. "During the last year the president of Wehr submitted two management recommendations to the board, one for the acquisition of a beer company, and one for the purchase of a controlling interest in an Italian affiliate in which Wehr owned roughly 25 percent. In the beer situation the division manager of the canned and frozen juices division identified, studied the merits, and recommended that the beer company be acquired. Its headquarters was near the division offices; the juice division included key executives with previous beer industry experience; the indicated price was attractive; several cents per share would be added to the Wehr earnings; and the consumer advertising requirements of the beer industry were understood by presently employed division executives.

"In accordance with established procedures, the possible

acquisition was discussed by the company's operating committee, which consisted of the chairman, the president, four divisional vice presidents and division managers, the vice president
of finance, and the vice president and general counsel. They
agreed unanimously to recommend to the board that the beer
company be acquired through the exchange of common stock.
Prior to the board meeting copies of a 10-page summary of a
staff study on the acquisition proposal were sent to the outside
board members. At the next regularly scheduled monthly meeting the president outlined the principal elements of the deal,
and the divisional vice president elaborated, especially under-
lining the advantages of the purchase.

"Discussion of the proposal was opened by an outside director
who wondered whether the beer business was the right kind of
a business for a predominantly food company to be in. Another
director raised doubts about the effects the acquisition of a
beer company would have on the Wehr Company's price/earn-
ings stock multiple, now considerably higher than those found
in the beer industry. Another suggested that the image of the
Wehr Company was almost unique and, to use his words,
perishable. There was a free, open, and challenging exchange
among the outside board members and key executives of management, and after two hours the consensus of the entire board
—insiders and outsiders—was that the beer company should not
be acquired.

"Shortly thereafter the Wehr Company's vice president international proposed to the company's operating committee that
the outstanding shares of an Italian joint venture enterprise be
purchased. Wehr owned 25 percent, and negotiations with the
Italian partners for the remaining 75 percent had settled the
price to be paid. To cope with the Italian partners' individual
tax problems, it was proposed and tentatively agreed to by
management that X common stock shares be issued for the
purchase price, but held in escrow over a five-year period.
Complete ownership of the Italian subsidiary would not be
transferred until the end of the five-year period, but the shares
of stock held in escrow would be distributed proportionately

at the end of each year, and any change in the market value would accrue to the Italian sellers.

"Again, this was approved by the company's operating committee and presented to the board for approval. And again, the outside directors discussed the issue thoroughly and declined to approve the proposed arrangement."

A vice president and inside director of the Wehr Company observed: "The board view prevailed all right. It would not go along with an arrangement that gave the appreciation between now and closing to those Italian gentlemen. If we set aside X number of shares now, if we continued to do well earnings-wise, and if the market went up, the ultimate value of our stock would be an enormous windfall to the sellers. I think our management really learned a lesson. This experience illustrates the need for an independent judgment by the board. No matter how good the president is, he is only one man, and he's got his limits. I don't care how able or broad he is, he can become an advocate for a viewpoint of division vice presidents."

• In another situation the chairman of the Rowe Company, who was also an outside director of the Acme Company, described a recent experience. "Let's take an example over at Acme. The management came in with a proposition of making an acquisition, and it was recommended without any qualification by management. It was picked apart by the board, and before the meeting was over everyone there agreed that it was just a bum deal. Nevertheless it was done in such a way that the chief executive officer and his people didn't feel that they hadn't been a part of the decision to change their minds. I have no use for board members who are abrasive and try to show up management. But I do think it is perfectly possible to sit down at a board meeting, have a discussion, and have the management go out with a different feeling than what they came in with. We have people on this board who have had a lot of experience in making business decisions of one kind or another, whether it happened to be in their particular field of expertise or not. They are in the habit of prying into the pro's and con's of issues, and they *are*, in fact, a critical element in the top management decision-making procedure."

A few, not many, situations were found in which boards of directors did in fact determine objectives, strategies, and policies.

ASKING DISCERNING QUESTIONS

The second generally accepted traditional and important role of the board is to ask discerning questions of the management. Research interviews indicate that in most companies directors at board meetings do not in fact ask discerning questions.

• "The board meeting," said one president, "is not a proper forum for discussion of questions by board members. You can't expect the president to expose all the pro's and con's of an issue at a meeting which subordinates attend. Also the board and management are not intended to be members of a debating society. You never end such a debate. You go on and on. And you get deeper and deeper in the damn thing. Sometimes you are in danger of starting a long debate or a controversy that just can't be settled. It's much better, if a board member does have a question, for him to raise it quietly with the president outside the meeting, and make arrangements to discuss his doubts with the proper people in the organization."

• Said the chairman of a large eastern company: "A board meeting is not a good place, relatively speaking, to raise questions. The reason is a sort of atmospheric reason. The fellow board member who has interest enough or knowledge enough to challenge the management with a perceptive question is probably very much in the minority. In most cases he is the one guy on the board who has some interest and feeling, and the rest of the characters on the board haven't read the material, don't know the business, can't make any sensible response with justification, and they are not really interested in getting into it."

Almost all the executives interviewed concluded that discerning questions should never be asked at a board meeting.

If challenging questions are to be asked, the usual suggestion was that the outside directors should telephone the president or arrange a luncheon with the president, or a subordinate designated by the president, to discuss outside the board meeting their questions, doubts, and concerns. The only circumstance under which discerning questions are appropriate at board meetings is when the outside director concludes there is a crisis situation in the management, and he either is prepared to or about to resign, or he believes that there is sufficient support from the other members of the board to oust the president. But it is only under the most crucial conditions, the preponderance of those interviewed believed, that discerning questions by outside directors are appropriate.

This executive point of view explains in part why board meetings in most companies are such meaningless exercises.

• One executive vice president described his board meetings as completely predictable, and his characterization typified essentially what I have found during the research interviews: "Before our one-hour monthly board meeting, I know exactly what is going to happen, and I know that the eight outside directors are not going to ask any questions. They may ask for clarification of some expressed position of the management, but that is all. Hell! I could write the minutes of the meeting before the meeting is held!"

• From the director's point of view, a reason given for not asking discerning questions was described as: "I, as an outside director, am unwilling to show my lack of a grasp of understanding of the problem or to display my ignorance. To be able to challenge the management with a discerning question, you've got to know enough really to be on fairly sound ground. Part of the problem is that you don't want to look like an idiot. And it's very easy to look like an idiot unless you spend enough time getting your facts in line and, you know, understanding what you're talking about."

"Professional courtesy" and "corporate manners" were phrases used to explain the lack of challenging questions.

• "If you have someone on your board with lots of experience abroad, say someone from IBM International, and management proposes to make an investment in _____, the outside director with experience could suggest that _____ is a lousy place to go. But a smart director won't say that. You don't say everything you think at a board meeting. There is a certain amount of professional courtesy involved if you are going to be a good director, and the same goes for management. An outside director takes a management on its batting average anyway. If 98 percent of the recommendations over a period of time have been good, and have worked out, and one comes along that you just disagree with, you don't make a federal case out of it—you may not even say anything, because you may be wrong."

• In one situation an outside director concerned about steadily declining earnings, and perceiving no apparent management program to reverse the trend, asked the chairman and the president what was being done to correct the situation. The other outside directors also expressed their concern, and the president, obviously embarrassed, responded with unpersuasive and unimpressive replies. After the meeting the chairman asked the initial questioner to stop by his office before leaving, and there he explained: "It is just plain bad manners to ask those kinds of questions in a board meeting. You must remember that you are challenging the president in the presence of his subordinates, some of whom are insiders on the board. If you have questions about what is being done to reverse the trend, the proper way is to make a date to confer with the president privately."

The manner in which questions are asked by board members was described by many presidents as the key.

• One said: "I want the outside directors to ask meaningful questions which perhaps will subtly challenge our plan, subtly challenge our strategy. I don't want to be asked questions that are just plain embarrassing, that are really asked to embarrass the management, or to highlight what should have been obvious in the area of management mistakes—because managements do continually make mistakes. I expect that in asking penetrating questions the knowledgeable outside director gives assurance to the management that he approves the actions that management is taking—even though management has not solicited specific approval. The president especially needs to achieve from the board some feeling that the board understands his problems, and that they are backing him in the actions that he is taking.

• "I have no time for an abrasive son-of-a-bitch. The manner in which a question is asked is all-important. A question asked in an abrasive manner tends to signal to the management and to the other members of the board that this particular board member disapproves of the way that management is conducting the business. Any abrasive or challenging question is almost a vote of no confidence. This is in the same category as criticizing your wife in public. If an outside director wants to telegraph that he has lost confidence in the chief executive officer, then the technique of asking an abrasive question at a board meeting is probably a very good one."

The statement by the president quoted above—that a challenging question, a discerning question, a question regarded as abrasive by the president constitutes in effect a vote of no confidence in him—was found to be a common point of view among most of the chairmen and presidents interviewed.

• In one case, for example, an outside director became concerned about the implications of speeches and press releases by the company president and, encouraged by other outside directors who shared the concern, he raised the issue with the president as gently as possible in a personal and private conversation. The president resisted any suggestion for a change in point of view or practice. At the next board meeting the outside director, believing he had the support of the other outsiders, raised the issue, and the president continued to refuse to change his position. A few months later proxy statement material for the annual election of directors was published, and the issue-raising outside director's name was not included on the current slate. The moral, he reported, was, "Don't raise questions with the president unless you can, for sure, count on the support of others on the board."

• A former outside director of a large industrial manufacturer reported on his efforts to ask discerning questions: "I had been a director of the company for about three years. It had grown rapidly, and one of America's basic industries was incorporating its control equipment into new construction as well as old facilities. To finance the company's increased needs for plant and working capital, the president chose to maintain the equity position of the company and to get the leverage advantage of term debt. After three consecutive quarter board meetings when approval had been asked for new debt arrangements, the next meeting included an agenda item on the same subject.

"At this meeting the president reviewed the financial operations for the period, which were excellent, and then requested board approval for another term loan. As I looked over the terms and studied the pro forma balance sheet, it did seem to me that we were approaching a debt/equity ratio higher than I thought appropriate. Incidentally, we had no bankers on the board. When the president asked for comments, I said, 'Bill, I've looked at what our balance sheet will look like after this borrowing, and looking ahead to the need for more capital for more expansion I wonder whether our debt/equity ratio isn't getting out of line.' The president's response was instantaneous. 'Damn it, John, I've been over this with our New York bankers, and if it's good enough for them, it sure as hell ought to be good enough for you.' This was not the first evidence of resistance to questions, and amounted to a climax incident for me. When I returned home the next day I wrote a letter of resignation from that board. Bill professed to, but really did not, want any challenging questions from the board. I have followed the company results since leaving, and it has done very well indeed. It is the industry leader in its field. Friends still on the board tell me, however, that Bill's attitude toward challenging questions remains the same."

• In another situation an outside director described his resignation from the board of a large western company as due completely to the president's response to the director's request for more information: "I asked questions about financial results and capital requests, and the new president brushed them aside. I talked with him privately about my interest and need for the data, and he thought these were not appropriate matters for the board. At the next meeting, which was about halfway through our fiscal year, I insisted that the board accept my resignation at that meeting. The president appeared a little shaken to have the issue raised at a board meeting, and asked me to withdraw the request and to wait until the end of the year when a new board would be elected. I decided that if I couldn't have answers to what I regarded as responsible questions, then I could not continue on the board. At that meeting my resignation was accepted, and later I received the usual board obit resolution: 'We express our appreciation for your X years of loyal and constructive service as a board member, and regret that it was necessary for you to resign. We wish you continued success . . .' and so on."

• An outside director of the Casey Company recounted a recent experience where he questioned the accounting policies employed at a year-end closing of the books. "The Casey Company is one of the leading medium-sized publishing and printing houses in the southeast. As the market has grown very well in that part of the country, and as more money was spent on school aid, the company did very well financially. Stock in the company was widely held and was listed on the American Exchange. I had been on the board only two years and knew, and know, relatively little about the book business. At our January 1970 board meeting, the estimated financial results for 1969 were presented by the president, who indicated that earnings per share would be two cents less than last year's. He added that in his judgment it was important to maintain the company's track record of increased earnings per share, and that conferences would be held with the company's public accounting firm to determine whether some changes in accounting procedures might enable finding four cents a share somewhere, so that an increase of two cents a share for the year could be reported.

"I raised a question as to the propriety of using accounting practices to accommodate the needs of earnings per share. The president suggested a special board meeting three weeks later, to which a senior partner of the accountants would be invited. Incidentally, we did not have an audit committee on the board. Three weeks later we met with the accounting firm partner, who stated that in his opinion it would not violate generally accepted accounting principles, and it would not require a footnote in the financial statements, to modify the basis of valuing the ending inventory of books in the process of manufacture, and to capitalize rather the expense of some start-up costs of a new plant which went onstream in the summer of 1969 in Mexico.

"Again I questioned the propriety and asked, 'If we were not looking for a few cents per share, would we consider different accounting practices?'—and the president's answer was negative. The meeting went on and on, and I finally had to leave to catch a plane in Atlanta for the flight home. Before leaving I said, 'I urge you not to change the basis of accounting; 1969 was a rough year economically, and if we come in with just two cents off last year, that is a damn good record. If I could stay, I would vote against these two adjustments.' The company's vice president and general counsel then said, 'Well, Sam, your skirts are clean if you leave before we vote the changes.' I said, 'Henry, don't offend me any more than you have. I'm not trying to duck a responsibility. I'm simply saying that if you want me to cast a ballot, I suggest we have a vote now, and mine is no. I must leave, and I urge you not to approve these changes because I think it's a mistake. This is friendly advice —I have nothing to gain.'

"The upshot of it was that as soon as I left they voted both changes, and the published report maintained the earnings curve. The president is a grand person, even though he doesn't want challenging questions. In his letter responding to my later resignation, he said that I had provided a significant service to the board, and asked whether there was any possibility that I might reconsider and rejoin the board."

Even friendly directors are turned aside on questions raised at board meetings.

• One said: "I have enormous respect for the president. He has done a phenomenal job in leading this company, but he simply does not have the time or the patience to include the board as an element of management. We get no written financial figures, we never approve capital expenditures—all I know is what I read in the annual report. A short time ago I asked at a board meeting what the amount of the investment credit would be for the year, and how many cents per share would be added to the earnings. The president brushed my inquiry aside when he said, 'That is a very difficult calculation to make, and anyway it doesn't really make any difference.' After the board meeting and before lunch a vice president came over and said, 'If you think you got an honest answer to your question about the investment credit, you are wrong.' My response was, 'Please don't think that *I* think that I got an honest answer.' "

Most of the presidents of the companies studied prefer not to have discerning or challenging questions asked by board members. There are, however, a few companies—a minority of case situations—in which the presidents not only tolerate questions but want them from their directors on almost any subject relevant to the business.

• One president, whose philosophy and attitude was confirmed by interviews with several board members of the company, said: "I think that unless you can expose what you are doing to questioning—unless you can honestly answer the questions that intelligent, informed men can ask—then you really aren't doing your job as president. Because sooner or later somebody is going to ask such questions. It could be at a stockholders' meeting, at a meeting with representatives from the investment banking community, or some investment advisory service, and you'll never have a chance to answer them, because they will answer the questions themselves. And especially in a business vested with the public interest like ours. You've got to be prepared with answers to even the most hostile questions. If you can't answer the questions that your own board members have been asking, you're going to have a hard time answering questions that, say, a hostile senator or a hostile student would ask. You've got to be prepared to answer these questions because basically, in this day and age, no business can survive unless it (a) is successfully managed for the shareholders, and (b) can demonstrate that it serves a balanced social purpose. You have to be able to answer questions related to that at all times. The day when you have a question arising in your board meeting that you can't answer—that you can't answer honestly and forthrightly, and be prepared to have your answer printed on the front page of the local newspaper, and be prepared to stand behind it—then you are in deep trouble. Of course a lot of businesses *are* in deep trouble today."

• A chairman of a large New York based company said: "I feel very strongly that if the top executive of a company can't take head-on directors' questions, constructive criticisms, or misplaced criticisms, he is not the right executive. He is trying to cover up something, or he's insecure, or he's trying to justify himself by pushing things under the rug. When we have board meetings here, I tell my insiders not to push problems under the rug—not to hold back on information so that there are surprises later. If you have a problem, I don't care how bad it is, put it on the directors' table. I just don't want to wake up all of a sudden some day and discover that a board of nondiscerning outside board members and I have really got a can of worms which we can't put back in the can.

"One of the outside directors said to me point blank recently that he wouldn't hang around unless he thought he could contribute, and he said that if he couldn't express himself and ask questions without resentment from the management, he wanted no part of the whole shebang. I told him that is precisely what we want."

• Another president noted: "If a management is willing to countenance the fact that you, as a board member, are likely to ask embarrassing questions, it says a lot about the management. It says the management is pretty damn competent."

• Said one president: "It takes an awful lot of guts for a board member to be on a board, see things he doesn't like, and then ask the pertinent and discerning questions of the management. Such men are rare birds indeed. It takes more guts than most people have. What they usually do is say, 'Life is too short, and I'll resign from the board.' Resigning, however, does not solve the company's problems—only that of the director who doesn't have the guts to stay."

Effect of Stock Ownership

In Chapter II, I presented the research findings of what directors do in large and medium-sized widely held corporations where the management and outside directors own little voting common stock. In this chapter, where the responsibility of outside directors to ask discerning questions of management is being examined, it is timely to report on a phenomenon which I observed during the field research period and during my years of active involvement in board functions. Outside board members who own or represent the ownership of substantial stock in the company are much more likely to ask discerning questions than an outside director who does *not* own stock, or at least not very many shares. Family trusts created in the past require trustees, who may be individuals or institutions and, in the case of the individual trustees, are likely to be invited onto or to negotiate a position onto the board of directors in which they represent substantial stock ownership. Institutional trustees typically do not seek or accept membership on the boards of companies in which they have substantial holdings —whether they should or not is a question apart from this study.

An avenue to a substantial stock interest in a listed company is the acquisition of a good-sized family-owned company. Frequently, as an element of the acquisition negotiations, one or two members of the family are assured of membership on the board. To these family members, positions on the board have prestige value, and it frequently turns out to be a condition for acquisition. In other cases the acquiring company's bylaws provided for cumulative voting, and the shares distributed to the family owners of the acquired company make it legally possible to assure at least one directorship, and in many cases two.

The trustees of family trusts have a standard of conduct and performance more legally defined than the standard of conduct and performance of the typical outside director. Some writers about boards of directors have suggested that corporate directors are in fact trustees for the company's stockholders. But this trustee-type standard has never been legally applied to the liability of corporate directors. The directors are not trustees; they are something else in the eyes of the law, and their performance standards are considerably less defined that those of trustees.

Family representatives on boards may or may not have trusteeship obligation, depending upon the circumstances of their family's affairs. But even if the family representatives are not bound to the legal status of trustees, the feeling of a family responsibility is real, and in many cases equal to or greater than that imposed by the law of trusts.

Directors in this position—with the legally imposed standards of trusteeship or with obligations to members of a family—were found to take a very active interest in the affairs of the corporation.

• In one instance the trustee-director, discouraged by the declining sales and profits of the company, arranged with the president to have a two-day session at the company headquarters to become better acquainted with its operations, and to get a better evaluation of the capacities of management to cope with the problems. On the second day he spent from 9:00 a.m. until midnight discussing with the president the conditions and policies of the company. Shortly after these conferences he said: "I had no idea how badly off this company is. It has lost its market share in its traditional businesses, and the recently acquired ventures are not panning out at all. There are unexposed and undisclosed liabilities, and implicit obligations to throw good money after bad in these ventures. These facts have not been communicated to the board at all. I spent fifteen hours with the president, and during that time he dodged, ducked, and came up with the most unresponsive answers you have ever heard. I am the trustee of a family trust that owns 5 percent of this company, and I cannot stand by and watch it go down the drain because of the shortcomings of an incompetent president."

The trustee-director then called the other outside directors, expressed his concern, and arranged a meeting to discuss what should be done. All nine outside directors of a board of fifteen were present, and after a three-hour discussion they agreed to direct the chairman to ask the president for his resignation. A few days later the usual form announcement was made: "The chairman of the XYZ Company announced today that Mr. John Jones, president, has resigned because of policy differences with the board. The chairman will assume the office of president and chief executive officer. Mr. Jones was not available for comment."

• A partner of a large financial institution in New York, commenting on this phenomenon, said, "I'm a director of three listed companies, and I find it most interesting to measure my attitudes as an outside director against those as a partner of this firm. You will notice that our quarters here in the Wall Street area are not what could be called posh, by any standards. You don't see a lot of modern or impressionistic art in the lobbies or the hallways. You won't find, if you look, any chauffeur-driven limousines of ours out on Broad Street. You won't find any collection of beautiful antique furniture in the partners' offices. And you won't find a company jet airplane parked over in Jersey. The reason is, this is my money. This is mine. And I don't want to see it wasted on unnecessary things. I feel like a real trustee to myself and my family. When proposals are made at partners' meetings to have a little more sumptuous quarters, on the ground that it will improve our image with our customers, I ask some real tough questions. Is it really necessary? What happens if we don't spend the money?

"When I go to the board meetings of the three companies I serve, that is not my property. I don't own more than 100 shares, and when I go along with management's request for approval of new leases on executive space on upper Third Avenue, or for approval of a larger jet airplane, I am not behaving as a trustee or an owner. I wonder what would happen if the full legal responsibilities of trusteeship were applied to all directors of American corporations. It is true, of course, that a handful of directors in the United States behave as if they were trustees, but there aren't many."

Sometimes the presence on the board of a major stockholder who believes one of his important functions as a director is to ask discerning questions encourages other outsiders to get involved in the questioning of the president.

• One chairman commented: "When the board includes an interested large stockholder who chooses to exercise his directorship muscle, the president can reasonably conclude that other outside directors will follow the example of the challenging director. We have such a director on our board, and we don't know of any way to get him off. Life would be a lot pleasanter if he would just quietly go away."

• In further elaboration of the point that substantial stock ownership by board members is conducive to the asking of discerning questions, the former president of a large chemical company owned by two other large companies as a joint venture stated: "The single most effective and best board of directors I have ever seen was the Dane Chemical board. The chairman and I were the two insiders, and there were five representatives from each of the two corporate owners. We met monthly, and you can be very sure the chairman and I were prepared for those meetings. The outside directors, as representatives of the owners, knew the industry, the competition, the manufacturing, marketing, and research problems, the pricing strategies. And they were involved. I don't mean they meddled in operating problems, but when we proposed to put $12 million into a plant and equipment for the production of an agricultural chemical, they spent the time to study the whole project and then approved the investment. It was not a rubber-stamp approval of management's recommendation. In my present company I could come up with a proposal to the board for a $12 million investment, and I probably wouldn't have three questions from the outside directors. And even the three questions wouldn't mean anything. Because they don't understand the business. I would have to be really off base before these people would challenge my recommendations."

SELECTING THE PRESIDENT

The third generally accepted traditional and important role of the board is to select the president. Research interviews and my personal experiences indicate that directors do not in fact select the president except under crisis conditions. The myth that the board selects the president has been eroding rapidly in recent years, even in the literature on the subject.

• One company vice chairman stated: "The old concept that the stockholders elect the board, and the board selects the management, is a fiction. It just doesn't apply to today's large corporations. The board does not select the management—the management selects the board."

• Another president stated: "The board neither selects nor de-selects the president."

Legal practice, of course, requires that the procedural amenities be observed, and shortly after every annual stockholders' meeting the newly elected directors assemble to approve the slate of officers for the coming year—an automatic approval of a slate submitted by the president. Also at this meeting of the new board it is customary to redesignate members of various committees of the board—executive, compensation, and audit.

The process by which new presidents are chosen for election at the annual stockholders' meetings, or between annual meetings, varied among the companies studied. But in most situations it was found that the controlling element in the naming of a new president is not the board of directors, but the person presently holding the title as president.

• One outside director said: "Whatever the president wants is what is going to be done."

• One executive vice president stated: "If our president were to retire in six months, his influence would amount, if I were guessing, to about 85 percent of the decision as to a successor. It would not be 100 percent. I don't think he could come to the board with someone they didn't know and say, 'Here's my successor.' But I do think that if he picked any one of our existing key executives, a fellow with a respectable record and some service with the company, the president's view would undoubtedly prevail."

• A president was asked who had selected him as the company's chief executive officer. He responded: "Oh, I kind of stumbled into that position I guess, after being around here long enough. The previous president, not the board, picked me.

On the other hand, I think it is important to recognize that he could not have picked me, or anyone else, without some reasonable degree of enthusiasm on the part of the board. But it isn't the board's job, initially, to go to the president and say, 'Look, we will pick the next number one man.' It's the other way around, with the board concurring."

• Another president stated: "The former company president tapped me to be president, and I assure you that I will select my successor when the time comes."

• Describing the involvement of the board in the selection of his successor, a president stated: "The board in this situation does not make the selection, but it performs a screening function. It serves as a sort of corporate conscience. There is a place for me to go with a recommendation. It's a place I've *got* to go, because I can't elect the president. I must convince a group of intelligent men that this is a sensible move. I've got interested people who will ask questions, and all the rest. In a very real sense the board is more of a safety valve rather than a body organized to make a formal decision."

A few situations were found in which board members informally discouraged presidents from nominating candidates as successors, but these were rare. The usual practice is for the president to designate and assure the election of the candidate of his choice.

In some companies a committee of the board, usually outsiders except for the president ex officio or officio, is charged with the responsibility of reviewing the performance, capability, and potential of executives inside the organization, and of being prepared, at any moment of time, to recommend who should be president. There can be great value in this approach, for it is one step in assuring that the problem of management succession is being looked at. In many companies the unexpected death of the president results in unthoughtful and sometimes frantic decisions when the exigency was not contemplated.

Also in these situations where the president has concluded that a suitable candidate for his successor cannot be found within the organization, and a search is initiated for possibilities outside the company, a committee of outside directors can be helpful to the president in interviewing and in evaluating the skills and abilities of candidates who, in most cases, are strangers. The task of choosing someone outside the company as president is a perilous one at best, and many presidents seek the advice and counsel of directors in the screening and selection process. It was found that presidents are much more likely to allow outside directors to participate in the presidential selection process when the candidates are outsiders than when they come from within the company.

Conclusions

Traditional literature on the functions of boards of directors includes the creation of corporate objectives, strategies, and broad policies as one of the most important functions, however defined—and the words used in describing this board function are subject to many different meanings. But research interviews in this study indicated that *most* boards do not peform the function. Indeed, management performs the function, and the board may or may not be involved in approving the policies, strategies, and objectives defined by corporate management. If the individual company practice is to secure board approval, the endorsement typically is perfunctory, and usually without challenging questions. For example, a management proposal for approval of an annual capital budget involving $10 million to $50 million or more will take roughly thirty minutes of a board meeting of one and a half hours. And it would be a rare board member who would do anything except go along with management. Paraphrasing one president's statement, "Nor *should* the board do anything except go along with management."

A few cases were found, however, in which the board did in fact take an active interest in the construction of company objectives, strategies, and policies. These were exceptional and not typical cases. In these companies there were situations where the board of directors did not go along with management, but rather through open discussion at the meeting developed a basis for turning back management's recommendations.

It was also found that in most companies, outside directors at board meetings do not in fact ask discerning questions. The board meeting is not regarded as a proper forum for the discussion of issues raised by challenging questions, and the board meeting should not be regarded as a debating society. Professional courtesy and corporate good manners also suggest that embarrassing questions not be asked, especially if some of the president's subordinates are inside board members. Any doubts or concerns about policies, operations, or management decisions are typically expressed to the president outside the meeting, unless the outside director is prepared to resign.

When questions are asked at board meetings by outside directors, presidents prefer that the questions be gentle, sympathetic ones which with subtlety may affect management decisions, but at the same time give assurance to the management of the outside directors' approval. Abrasive, challenging, and discerning questions were not regarded as appropriate at board meetings. Most presidents regarded the asking of such questions as a vote of no confidence.

Expression by top executives that abrasive questions symbolize a vote of no confidence in the president suggests that "unless you agree with everything I propose, you don't have confidence in the management." No managements

were found during this research study, nor during my years
of study and involvement in top management structures,
that never made mistakes—mistakes that in some instances
might have been avoided by the participation of an interested and responsible directorate. No corporate president is
always right.

The feeling by top executives that an abrasive question
is tantamount to a vote of no confidence reminds one of
the husband who at dinner says, "Dear, isn't the steak over-
cooked?" and the wife's response is, "You don't love me
any more."

There are some presidents, however, though in a minority of the companies studied, who *do* want the outside
board members to ask discerning, challenging, or abrasive
questions. Such a president believes that he is indeed only
one man, and though he is supported by a staff of skilled
specialists, there is something to be gained by having the
involvement of outside directors.

Also a few outside directors were found who do ask discerning questions at and outside the board meetings. These,
as one interviewee said, "are rare birds indeed."

What is perhaps the most common definition of a function of the board of directors—namely, to select the president—was found to be the greatest myth. The board of
directors in most companies, except in a strict legal and
operationally meaningless procedure, and except in a crisis,
does not select the president. The president usually chooses
the man who succeeds him to that position, and the board
complies with the legal amenities in endorsing and voting
his election.

There is considerable merit in the practice of a president's selecting his own successor with what amounts to
almost automatic approval by the board. The president
knows, through the experience of day-to-day working relationships with his subordinates, which of them has the

capacities and potential to succeed him. There is no one in the organization better able to evaluate the capacities of key subordinates. Also he knows from experience what the unique requirements are for his own job, and therefore he is in the best possible position to match candidates with job requirements. Certainly board members, with relatively brief exposures to possible candidates, and then under almost synthetic and staged conditions, are not able to exercise informed judgments on the relative merits of possible candidates for the presidency. The board, it was found, does serve as the final approving agency, but rarely indeed does it disapprove the recommendations of the president.

CHAPTER IV

The Powers of Control

To determine today's meaning of the legal language describing the board's function—"the business shall be managed by a board of at least three members"—we have examined in the last chapter three traditional, generally accepted, and important definitions of board roles: (1) establishing basic objectives, corporate strategies, and broad policies; (2) asking discerning questions; and (3) selecting the president. It was determined that in most situations boards of directors do *not* perform these three functions; these roles are fulfilled by the president. Further it was found that two critical factors determine what a board of directors of any size of company, and with any distribution of stock ownership, does in fact do "to manage the enterprise": (1) are the powers of control in the president; and (2) with the powers of control in the president, how does he choose to exercise them? These factors will be examined in this chapter.

LOCATION OF THE POWERS OF CONTROL

In the small family corporation where the ownership of the stock and the management are identical, we have the simplest and clearest identification of the location of the powers of control. It is, of course, with the family owners. In these cases the board of three usually consists of husband, wife, and the family attorney.[1] Some small company own-

---

[1] See *The Board of Directors in Small Corporations*, p. 12

ers, to multiply the sources of management know-how and knowledge available to the president, add outside board members. Anyone with experience as an outside director of such a small family enterprise recognizes that the role of the outside board member in this circumstance is at most advisory. The family owners possess de jure powers of control and they determine what board members do or do not do.

At the other end of the corporate galaxy from the family company amoeba is the very large, widely held enterprise in which the management and members of the board individually own little voting stock. The de jure powers of control derived from ownership is fractionated and dissipated among thousands of stockholders. In this situation the powers of control usually rest with the president—not with the board, and not with the stockholders of the company.

Powers of control mean the powers to exercise virtually all the rights of ownership. In terms of company operations, the powers of control held by managements of large, widely held companies are the same as the powers of control held by the owner-managers of a small family company. In the large enterprise the powers of control typically rest in the president, not in the unorganized and essentially unorganizable stockholders. In the small company which is owner-managed, the owner-managers exercise de jure powers of ownership. In the large company, with the absence of control or influence by the widely dispersed owners, the president has the de facto powers to control the enterprise. It is the president who, like the family owner-managers in the small corporation, determines in large part what the board of directors does or does not do.

Many writers and observers have noted this phenomenon. Among these is Edward S. Mason:

Control has passed from ownership hands into the hands of management; management personnel is more highly specialized and selected for professional competence; its motivations are substantially different from those of the owner-capitalist; and its area of discretionary action and the character of the limitations that bound their area differ markedly from those relevant to the enterprises of an earlier capitalism. There is some reason, therefore, to characterize this supposed transformation of American capitalism by the term 'managerial.'[2]

John Kenneth Galbraith, in *The New Industrial State*, said:

The men who now run the large corporations own no appreciable share of the enterprise. They are selected not by the stockholders but, in the common case, by a Board of Directors which narcissistically they selected themselves.[3]

Adolf A. Berle and Gardiner C. Means pointed out in 1932 that the stockholders' right to vote by proxy actually was a tool to reduce or eliminate their powers of control.

It has been observed that under the original corporate situation there was a large amount of residual control in the shareholding group. A weakening of this control is a study by itself; only the major steps can be noted here. We are here concerned with that branch of the corporate power which had primarily to do with carrying on the business for which the concern was organized. The direct manifestation of the shareholder's power in this regard was and is his right to vote.

This begins to weaken with the right to vote by proxy. Designed probably as a convenience to the absent shareholder, it was a century ago denied to the shareholder save where by

---

[2] Edward S. Mason, "The Apologetics of 'Managerialism'," *The Journal of Business*, January 1958, p. 1.

[3] John Kenneth Galbraith, *The New Industrial State*, Boston, Houghton Mifflin, 1967, p. 2.

special provision it was inserted, but its apparent convenience speedily led to the inclusion of this right in every charter or in the appropriate section of the corporation act. The growth of corporations, the dispersion of shareholders, the manifest impossibility for the vast majority of shareholders to attend meetings, have made the right to vote, in reality, a right to delegate the voting power to someone else—and the proxy is almost invariably a dummy chosen either by the management, by the "control" or by a committee seeking to assume control. The proxy machinery has thus become one of the principal instruments not by which a stockholder exercises power over the management of the enterprise, but by which his power is separated from him.[4]

Between the two extremes of corporate size—between the family company where management is ownership and control, and the very large company where management is not ownership but control—there are a wide variety of power centers, power influences, and power structures. The variations are so numerous that some students of boards of directors have concluded that it is impossible to generalize about board activities—each corporate situation is different. There are large and medium-sized companies in which family members of management who once controlled from 51 to 100 percent of the ownership now control 1 to, say, 25 percent of the ownership; even with their sharply reduced proportion of ownership, they are able, through tradition and influence, to control the management as if they owned the entire company.[5] There are other companies in which a representative of a family trust holding, say, 10 percent of the voting stock has the powers of control and thereby

---

[4] Adolf A. Berle and Gardiner C. Means, *The Modern Corporation and Private Property*, New York, Macmillan, 1932, pp. 128, 129.

[5] The distinctive problems of members of the board of directors of family-controlled or tightly-controlled companies will be discussed in Chapter VIII.

makes, or influences the making of, the critical strategy decisions for the company.

In other companies the presence on the board of a person who owns or represents the ownership of a substantial block of stock sometimes diminishes the presidents' complete powers of control. It was found that some representatives of ownership on the board spent considerable amounts of time working as directors and were involved in all major management decisions. Others, however, were passive, compliant, non-involved, and did not challenge the presidents' powers of control. Analysis of the situations did not identify critical factors which would enable any dependable prediction of whether a stockholder director would play an active or a passive role. The dynamics of the balancing of powers of control and the flow of powers of control of large enterprises is worthy of further study.

Companies vary with regard to the location of power, and the significant point is that what directors do or do not do is determined in large part by whether the power is in the company presidency, in one or more members of the board of directors, or in any one or more combination of hundreds of divisions of power between the presidency and the board. There are even situations where the powers of control are in neither the president nor the board, but in some influential non-officer stockholder.

In the large or medium-sized company the powers of control of the enterprise typically are in the president. In these situations it is the president who determines what the members of the board do or do not do. Bernard J. Bienvenu wrote:

Although the capacity and interest of directors are strong factors in determining the status of the board in the corporation, management usually decides the role that the board will assume.[6]

Another observer, E. Everett Smith, stated:

. . . For all practical purposes the board is a creature of the chief executive. He alone can structure it in terms of his attitude toward its function, the types of problems brought before it, and the manner in which material is presented to it. As a practical matter he can, although not always without difficulty, change the make-up of the board and select new members.

In the final analysis, I believe the basic cause for the decline of the board is the fact that many chief executives are not really convinced they want a strong and independent group of directors. I realize that this is not a popular statement; but based on the privilege of considerable observation, I do believe it is an accurate expression of the problem in many companies. And is it not a natural situation? After all, the chief executive has fought long and hard to reach his position of power. Is it not normal and natural for him to tend to avoid critical review of his stewardship?[7]

The controlling influence of the president in the determination of what directors do or not do was illustrated by many of the discussions during my field research.

• The chairman of a large eastern company said: "An awful lot of what directors do is a function of the temperament of the president. Is the president the kind of a guy who looks for as many inputs as he can get on major decisions, or does he pretty much operate on the basis, 'I know the answers, so don't, Mr. Directors, get in my way.'? You can very quickly tell whether the president is prepared to invite questions, to listen, to think

---

[6] Bernard J. Bienvenu, "Board of Directors Revisited," *Business Horizons,* Fall 1962, p. 44.

[7] E. Everett Smith, "Put the Board of Directors to Work," *Harvard Business Review,* May–June 1958, p. 43.

about the other points of view, and to react responsibly to them. The whole thing turns on the president's attitude. His attitude reflects itself. It builds. And the president who enlists the assistance of interested directors is a president who builds an organization inside based on participation. This relationship similarity is interesting—the team of subordinates has got to be the team of the chief executive, and the team of the board has to be the kind of a team with whom he can have a mutual and effective working relationship. I tried to build a team at the subordinate level, and at the board level, when I was president. My successor, with another style of management, with a different perception of what he regards as the critical problem areas in the company, will build his own team of board members. He just damn well doesn't have the power to change directors immediately, but he has increasing power to change as time goes on. He then will throw off the board those directors who can't, or won't, go along with his ideas. The president has to feel his way until he is satisfied that he can in effect dominate a majority of the board."

• Another top executive stated: "To put it bluntly, whether a board has any function or not, it must truly reflect the nature of the chief executive officer of the company more than anything else. If he wants to use the board, he will use them. And if he doesn't want to use the board, he will run over them pretty roughshod. Basically the board can be made just about as useful as the president wishes it to be."

• "The president of a company, or the chairman of the board, or whoever runs this operation, really determines the contribution the board makes. If all he wants to do is to get up in front of them and sort of go through some motions, see that fees get distributed, give them a bit of lunch—then that's the kind of performance you will get, because the chief executive officer controls the affair. If, on the other hand, the chief executive officer seeks out where in the management areas various board members might be able to make more of a contribution than in others, and then structures his board so that emphasis is placed on such questions rather than on the rote alternative, then the chief executive officer is making a direct impact on the contribution the board makes. This, I suppose, is a matter of style."

• Another example of the president's powers of control was cited by an executive vice president of a large southern company. "The old man has exactly the kind of a board he wants. They all live here in the city, and they just don't do a damn thing as directors. The old man thinks it is a great board, and from his point of view he is probably right. From my point of view they are a big glob of nothing. Not that there aren't some extremely able outsiders on the board—there are. But as board members, they know who is in control and they will never cross the old man."

This point of view was confirmed many times during the study.

• One example was provided by a director, an executive vice president: "What any new board member finds out very quickly in our company is that it is very difficult to do anything except go along with the recommendations of the president. Because directors who don't go along with them tend to find themselves asked to leave."

EXERCISE OF THE POWERS OF CONTROL

It was found that most presidents, completely aware of their powers of control, chose to exercise the powers in a manner which was moderate and acceptable to their peers on the board. Typically, efforts were made by presidents to help self-respecting directors feel that they were performing useful functions while at the same time indicating to them that their role was limited largely to advice and counsel.

Presidents, it was found, are aware that outside board members are usually extremely busy people, and they tailor the agenda and the flow of data to permit the directors to feel that they are involved in major company problems to a reasonable and appropriate extent.

• One president stated: "My board members are well-known and distinguished business leaders of other companies. I am delighted to have them on the board. But they know, and I know, that they don't have the time to really understand our company, the industry, the product line, the competition, and so on. I do want them to feel that they are making a contribution, and I want them to be sufficiently motivated to stay on the board. One thing I do is to take the board members and their wives to Europe every year for a week, in the spring. We charter a jet airplane, arrange a not too strenuous schedule which permits visits to some of our plants, and then we play golf or do the museums in the afternoons. Later in the year, when we have a capital appropriation to enlarge the factory, say, in Spain, the directors can remember, 'Oh yes, we visited there last year.' Also the overseas key employees like to see me and dine with the directors and their wives. It's good for their morale. The delicate role of the president is to enable self-respecting directors to feel that they are doing something useful as directors, while at the same time he is maintaining his control of the management of the enterprise. The amount of time our directors have to spend on our company does not permit them to have any real understanding of our problems. But they do get exposed to enough so that they do not look stupid."

Also communicated to, and generally accepted by, directors was the fact that the president possessed the complete powers of control. Those members of the board who elected to challenge the presidents' powers of control were advised, usually outside the board meetings, that such conduct was inappropriate or they were asked to resign.

• In one company, for example, the chairman commented on the behavior of his successor as president: "I had been president of the Kane Company for fifteen years, and with the board's approval selected a vice president to succeed me as president and chief executive officer. I always had a good working relationship with the company's outside board members, although it was perfectly true that if any issue came down to the wire—which it rarely did—my point of view would prevail. It was no secret that I controlled the board and the company. When the new president took over I stayed on as chairman and tried very hard—and succeeded—in not meddling with his approach to taking over and managing the business.

"After about six months of his administration, one or two of the outside directors, old friends of mine, came to me and said they were worried about the manner in which the president pushed aside suggestions by the board and discouraged discussion on any topic at the board meetings. I told him that the president had a different manner and a different approach to his job, and that I had promised myself not to interfere in any way in the approach he took. A few months later the president believed that he was offended, insulted, and threatened by a question asked by an outside board member, and promptly asked for his resignation. The president asked me to visit with the offending director, and I did. I said to the director that he and I as a previous president had the right chemistry in our relationship, but it was clear that the same chemistry didn't carry over with the new president. I told him that it was always impossible to forecast what power will do to a newly elected president's behavior; that the president was feeling and exercising a power he had never had before; that the president was bright, emotional, and absolutely persuaded that the outside director should resign. Before I left his office, he agreed to yield to the new president's exercise of power and to resign from the board."

Some presidents, and these were dramatic exceptions to the moderate behavior of most, know that they control the enterprises, regard the boards of directors as at best a necessary legal appendage, and flaunt their powers of control.

• As described by a director of one company: "The president is about as personally offensive to outside directors as he can be. The only reason I put up with him is that a lot of people think that this is a large high-prestige company." The president himself observed that the board was not really necessary, performed no function, and "It might be a good idea not to pay the directors, but rather to charge them a fee for the prestige of being on the board of a large and successful company."

• Not quite such flagrant presidential style of exercising power was found in a large midwestern company. Here, the president selected a board consisting of seven outsiders and four insiders; meetings were held quarterly and never lasted more than one hour. The outside board members were chairmen or presidents of well-known companies, and most of the outsiders shared the president's interest in golf. Board meetings consisted of a review of financial results of the period, and the presentation of management's requests for approval of capital appropriations, which were automatically voted without any questions from the board. Immediately prior to adjourning the meeting the president usually asked outside board members to comment on economic conditions in their respective industries, whereupon the meeting was adjourned.

An outside board member of this company observed: "The president is an extremely able executive, and the record of growth and earnings of his company are impressive. He is an old, old friend for whom I have the greatest respect. He knows the business, the industry, the competition, and has done a superb job of anticipating industry changes. But he does regard the trappings of the corporation as more of a hindrance than a help."

Similar attitudes as to the role of boards were expressed by the chief executive officers of other large companies.

• One stated: "I didn't get to be president by soliciting a lot of opinions, then getting a consensus of everybody around, and going along with the majority—and that's one of the reasons our board has never really shaped up."

• Another, when asked what he wanted from his board stated: "Hell, I don't want anything from them except to go along and agree with me."

The case situations cited above are, to be sure, extreme and flagrant examples of a style and exercise of the powers of control by company presidents. In my study of corporations they are not typical, but rather constitute a small minority of the situations in the companies sampled.

An equally small fraction of situations were found in which the president's attitude was at the other extreme from that of the "tyrant." A few presidents, although acknowledging that theoretically they might exercise strongly the powers of control of the business, accepted the classical concept of board authorities and responsibilities to the stockholders. The presidents wanted board involvement in determining company objectives, strategies, and policies; they welcomed as constructive the discerning and penetrating questions of outside board members; and they assumed that in many areas, such as the selection of the president and executive compensation, the board was a decision-making body. But in the total sample these too constituted a very small minority of the situations in the companies studied.

Conclusions

Owner-managers of small corporations possess and exercise de jure powers of control because ownership is management. Owner-managers, therefore, determine what directors do or do not do. In large and medium-sized, widely held companies ownership is spread and dissipated among thousands of stockholders whose powers of ownership, while theoretically equivalent to those of the small company owner-managers, are actually minimal and almost non-existent. Presidents of these companies have assumed and do exercise the de facto powers of control of the companies for which they are responsible. To them the stockholders constitute what is in effect an anonymous mass of paper faces. Thus, presidents in these situations determine what directors do or do not do.

Sometimes the presidents' complete powers of control may be reduced or influenced by the presence on the board of a large stockholder or the representative of a large stockholder. Analysis of these companies resulted in the identification of no factors by which to predict limitations on the presidents' complete powers of control.

Most presidents, it was found, choose to exercise their powers of control in a moderate and acceptable manner with regard to their relationships with boards of directors. They communicate, though, explicitly or implicitly, that they, as presidents, control the enterprises they head, and this is generally understood and accepted by the directors. Many of them are presidents of companies themselves, and they thoroughly understand the existence and location of powers of control.

A few situations were found in which presidents in the exercise of their powers of control behaved in a tyrannical manner and regarded their boards as necessary but unimportant legal appendages to the corporate structure. Also, a few cases were found in which presidents, aware of their complete powers of control, chose to treat boards as major and important elements in the management process. These presidents thought of boards as truly representatives of stockholders and insisted (1) that board members become involved in the determinations of objectives, strategies, and policies, (2) that directors ask challenging and discerning questions, and (3) that boards should select and evaluate the performance of company presidents. These presidents, like the tyrants mentioned above, were found to constitute a small minority in the instances studied.

CHAPTER V

Criteria for Selection and Motivation of Directors

I^N the first four chapters I reported that most boards serve as sources of advice and counsel to presidents, provide some sort of discipline for managements, and are available in the event of a crisis. I found, also, that most boards do not determine objectives, strategies, and broad policies, ask discerning questions, and select and evaluate the president. Thus, boards were found *not* to perform the classical and generally accepted roles that are attributed to them.

The disparity between the myths of what directors should do as described in business literature and the realities I found during field studies is caused by company presidents choosing to permit boards to perform only relatively limited advisory roles and not to become involved in policy making and other frequently identified functions. Boards do not do more than they do because presidents do not want them to do more.

Presidents with de facto powers of control generally determine the membership and composition of boards of directors, and in this chapter I report on who serves on boards, how directors are selected, and why they are willing to serve other companies in the capacity of a director.

OUTSIDE DIRECTORS WITH PRESTIGIOUS POSITIONS

In large and medium-sized companies the outside directors are usually leaders in their profession or industry. A review of the proxy statements of such companies discloses an impressive list of prestigious names of prestigious companies, investment banking firms, commercial banks, law firms, and academic institutions. On the boards of larger companies are found the top executives of these institutions, and as the prestige and size of the company diminish, so do the ranks and titles of those who serve as outside directors.

Most of the presidents interviewed stated that among the qualifications of candidates to serve as outside directors, position and title as leaders in their field were essential.

• One president said: "We have a standing rule that no one can be an outside director in our company who is not the top person in his organization. If he isn't, he can't be on our board. I don't care how able he is; our board as now constituted has top men as outsiders, so any replacements over the years have got to be their peers. You can't downgrade the prestige of our board membership by inviting, say, a promising vice president to serve as a board member."

• Another president said: "As head of my company I get a considerable number of invitations to serve as an outside board member of other organizations. I just can't take on any more. But when I regret, and suggest one or more of our key vice presidents, the matter is dropped, and neither the vice presidents nor I ever hear from them again. It is perfectly clear that their only interest is in the title and not in the man. Now, some companies have to accept less—they just don't draw the top names. But you'd be surprised at how, whatever their position, they always shoot for the top man."

• The executive vice president of a large chemical company

observed: "I came to this company about three years ago as executive vice president and director, from the presidency of a medium-sized manufacturing company in the midwest. As president of that company I had innumerable requests to serve on other company boards—big banks, insurance companies, large industrial and manufacturing companies scattered throughout the midwest. I served on a couple, just because the presidents were close friends. When I moved east and took this job as executive vice president of a company five times the size of my former company, invitations to serve on boards ceased. I was attractive and desirable as an outside director when I was president, but now that I am only an executive vice president, there is no more attraction. Yet I am the same person, with more experience, but not desirable."

• Another facet of the preoccupation with having only prestige-type and top names as outside directors was disclosed in a personal experience of my own in the early 1960s. The president of a large manufacturing company, with a vacancy on his board and a proxy statement to prepare, asked me for names of talented and qualified candidates. I suggested the name of a 40-year-old former student who is bright and able, and at that time was vice president of finance of a very large manufacturing company in the east. I reported that this man had progressed rapidly, and I would guess that he would become president of his organization in four or five years. The response of the president was: "But how can I be sure? If he is not made president of his company, we have made a mistake, and bet on the wrong man. We just can't take the chance. I will keep him in mind, and if he does get to be president, I hope we can add him to our board then."

• "Presidents and chairmen of large and respected companies enjoy the prestige of serving on similar large and respected company boards. They are identified with their peers. They find the experience socially satisfying. Outside directorships provide a few more lines in their *Who's Who*, and it is a little bit like being knighted to say, 'I'm a director of General Motors, or General Electric, or AT&T.' "

• The president of a west coast company stated: "You've got to remember that the outside directors of large national and regional companies are members of a sort of club. To be considered for admission to the club you must have the title as president or chairman of a respectable and respected organization. This is what some young people call the Establishment. But these are the people you do business with, travel around with, serve on community projects with—and it has to be a group the members of which get along together. Regionally each area has its elite. Sometimes many will in fact be members of the same golf or social club. Here in Los Angeles you will find a great number of directors with membership in the Los Angeles Country Club; in Cleveland the same is true of the Union Club—each city has its hard core members of the club group."

• John Bunting, president and chief executive of First Pennsylvania Banking and Trust Company, Philadelphia's largest bank, has a different philosophy. He was quoted in the *Wall Street Journal*[1] as saying: "The idea that only 100 people in Philadelphia are capable of holding all the important corporate and civic boards in the city may have been sound years ago, but it's certainly no longer justifiable." Mr. Bunting, who serves on the board of two other corporations and no less than twelve civic, charitable, and nonprofit institutions, stated: "There are any number of qualified people today who want a piece of the action, and shouldn't be frozen out of participating." Mr. Bunting was contemplating turning as much as a third of the bank's directorships over to representatives of consumers, young adults, employees, blacks, poor people, and militant feminists.

The majority of those interviewed during the research expressed the judgment that the prestige of the outside director was a critical element among the qualifications desired for directorship.

---

[1] August 5, 1970, p. 14.

• "A man's stature in the business community is, I think, very important. It is important to all the stockholders in that they are given confidence that they don't have a bunch of stooges or stumble-bums who are representing them in the management of the company. Also, knowledgeable financial people, in talking about a company, refer to the board as indication of the caliber of the company—the management of a company is judged by the kind of board people that they select and keep."

• "The board is part of the image of the company. The caliber and stature of the outside board members, both just as names and as people circulating in the business community, contributes to the image of the company. When I look at a company, I look at who is on the board. I don't know how good a criterion it is, but I form a judgment—is this a responsible kind of outfit, or is it a marginal high-flyer? The type of people on a board does, in a series of informal and intangible ways, have a good deal to do with what the character of a company is. Is it a respectable and conservative company, or is it highly speculative? The investing public, you know, really cares who is on the board."

• "You've got to have the names of outside directors who look impressive in the annual report. They are, after all, nothing more or less than ornaments on the corporate Christmas tree. You want good names, you want attractive ornaments. You want to communicate to the various publics that if any company is good enough to attract the president of a large New York bank as a director, for example, it just *has* to be a great company."

• The president of a large company with extensive international operations observed: "In the United States the prestige of the outside directors is a marginal value. But when you go to Europe and talk to one of the big banking firms, and you can say you have a major U.S. top bank officer on your board, you point out that here is a recognized banker on our board and therefore you can understand the caliber of company that we are. In Europe they look at things a little differently, where banks own so much of the stocks of business. There are a lot of interlocks, and they appreciate seeing a well-known banker on our board."

A minority of those interviewed stated that the title, stature, and reputation of outside directors were relatively unimportant as credentials for good outside board members.

• "I'm not interested in—none of us in the company is interested in—people because they have a prestige name. If you say that the job of the management of a company is to make a success of it, and to get a reasonably good multiple on the company's shares, I don't think that having a lot of important names on the board is very important. The important thing is to have the right people. Maybe if you had an unknown company, then it might be helpful to have a prestige-name kind of a fellow on the board. But when you are dealing with a well-known publicly held company with a reputation for integrity on its own, it just is not important to have a lot of fancy names. The only thing that really counts is how well the company is doing, and what the investment community thinks of its management."

• "Unless a company is in trouble financially or from a management point of view, or has an internal fight for control going on, or something breaks out in the newspapers and becomes the talk of the town—stockholders, investors, analysts could not care less who is on the board."

• A president said: "To me, titles and impressive names are pretty shallow, because if we are not doing a good enough job to attract the acceptance and confidence of the financial community on our own, I don't care what names you put on the board—the company isn't going to last very long. I've had some top names in the past, but very honestly they don't mean a thing. It might be window-dressing to the financial community, but they aren't really impressed by names—it doesn't mean anything."

Top Executives Are Busy People

A not surprising finding of the research was that top executives are exceedingly busy people. Fitting the research interviews into their clogged schedules was a small indication of their time problems, and this was confirmed in almost every discussion.

- One president observed: "I don't do much as an outside director. I know I should do more, but the facts of life are that the other outside directors and I have full-time jobs with a lot of responsibilities to our respective companies. The problem is not the lack of motivation because of the low fees—the problem basically is that I've got more than I can do right here on this job. Presidents of large companies are busy people, with careers that typically occupy 110 percent of their working hours. And they have a primary set of responsibilities. They and I tend to look at outside directorships as being an extra burden. It certainly doesn't have the same importance in their priority list as the primary job they have, so naturally it gets less attention. The reason I don't get involved, as an outside board member, is that I don't have time to get the facts, and I prefer not to look stupid. Silence is a marvelous cover."

- "Running a big complicated corporation is a full-time job that takes 150 percent of your time and capacity. It is no job for dilettantes. You can't possibly keep abreast of what goes on in your company and in someone else's as well. Company presidents, by the nature of their job, just should not try to serve as outside directors of other companies."

- The president of a large eastern company stated: "I am on the Lang board as an outside director, but that is the only one, and the reason is historical. I have not accepted invitations to be on other boards because I have a pretty full-time job right here."

- The president of another company, commenting on the work done by his prestige-named outside directors, said: "These people are on the board primarily as a favor to me. They don't have time to do their homework. One of them had to resign recently from the board of one of this country's largest companies. He said that it was a most interesting association and he regretted that he had to resign because of a product-line conflict. He said the problems of the company were fascinating because of their size. He said also that he couldn't make any contribution because he didn't have the time to have even the beginnings of a small understanding of the problems."

• Another president said: "I don't see how we are going to lick the problem of getting the time of the kinds of people— presidents of other companies—that we normally reach out for as directors. They are heads of their own big enterprises and barely have time to brush their teeth. Also, these outside-director presidents don't get involved, because there is sort of an unwritten code—they don't want outside directors bothering them in their operations, and therefore they don't bother the management of companies they serve as outside directors. By 'bothering operations' I mean understanding enough about the company and industry to be able to ask some sensible questions."

A few situations were found in which company presidents, sensitive to the high priority of their primary responsibilities to their own company, prescribed a company policy forbidding any executive from serving as an outside director of other companies.

• One said: "Our top people are paid well, and nothing less than their total time and energy is expected. If they get interested and involved as outside directors, inevitably they are solving other people's problems, not ours."

• The dilemma was described by the president of a large company in this way: "The ideal outside director is a relatively young man, full of vinegar, willing to devote his time and efforts to helping you in any way you ask him. It could be in giving his advice on major company problems, help in sales, help in government matters. But he can't do this in one hour a month. If the fellow is the head of a large company he is looking for the same thing, and he can't give you more than one hour a month. If the fellow is younger and down the line in the organization, he can't spend the necessary time away from the job—he won't be allowed by his company to be away. It's a real dilemma."

SELECTION OF OUTSIDE DIRECTORS
BY THE PRESIDENT

In large and medium-sized companies, the powers of control—the de facto powers of ownership—are in the president. It was found that in these situations it is the president who selects new outside members of the board, and it is the president who de-selects existing outside board members when nominations for the board are necessary for annual stockholders' meetings.

• "The theory," as one president expressed it, "is that if a president is doing a good job for the stockholders, who is better qualified to select the board members than he is?"

• The president of a large eastern company said: "Just as a president must create an effective team and working relationships with his subordinates, so he must create also his effective team of outsiders on the board of directors. There is a great deal in common in these two teams. The president wants people on both teams who can work together constructively in the interest of the corporation. In my company, and in every company I know about, the president, when the question of a vacancy on the board arises—including the making of a vacancy—is the person who makes the selection of the new director, fundamentally. He makes the selection. Now, he probably will discuss the candidate's qualifications with the present board members, but the president is trying to build his team on the board, and therefore it must be his basic decision. The average driving chief executive attaches an awful lot of importance to having his men on the board. If he is smart, he will approach the other directors with his recommendation and go through the formalities of getting their participation, but it is not very real. You see, it is the management that is self-perpetuating. The officers of a company are even required by SEC procedures to say who will be proposed as directors."

The procedure and courtesy of soliciting the support and vote of existing board members by the president was found to be common among the situations studied, although there were a few examples of unilateral decision making by presidents without coordination.

• One chairman said: "I select the new board members, but I always get the concurrence of the present board. It's a sort of center club—the members vote for, or blackball, candidates for admission. So far they have never blackballed any of my recommended names."

• Another president stated: "Once I have decided on the man who should be our new board member, I discuss this informally outside of board meetings with our three-man committee of the board that officially nominates people to the board. Then I mention the man's name at our board meeting—say, in September—and suggest that the board members think over the man's qualifications. At the October meeting the nominating committee puts the man's name up for election. Rarely would I submit a man's name for board membership and ask for it to be voted on at the same meeting."

Most executives interviewed confirmed that the selection of new directors was controlled and decided by the president. Among the many statements made were:

• "During the last five years all new directors have been selected by the president."

• "They are really friends of mine, these guys, these outside directors. They are people I selected to be on the board. And they are on the board because I personally asked them to be on the board."

• A staff vice president of a large southern company stated: "I'm not trying to say that the outside board members are not men of stature and ability. I am saying the board is the president's board—*his* team of outsiders."

It was found that in those situations in which the president's de facto powers of control were counterbalanced by the presence of one or more directors on the board who owned or represented the ownership of substantial blocks of stock, these directors actively participated in the selection of new directors. The control powers of the president were not complete.

• The president of a large company, who was also trustee of a family trust holding stock in a nationally known manufacturing company, and who was on its board, stated: "I'm chairman of an ad hoc committee of the board to nominate new members for election to the board. The president is not on the ad hoc committee. We want people on the board who have established their records as able citizens, as leaders in their field, who, you can say, are studious types capable of analyzing and reacting to problems; and we are looking for help at this level. For example, the last director added was president of a large company with a record in growing through acquisitions. We need that thinking. Four of us on the board are going to develop a committee of the board, including the new man, to force the management to get more active than they have been in this area. I think it is very important. The president has been so wrapped up in his own business that he hasn't really looked outside his product-line blinders."

Some situations were found in which substantial shareholdings among the outside directors did not constitute any sort of counterbalance to the president's powers of control. Potentially or latently influential directors, for any one of a variety of reasons, did not chose to employ their strength as owners, and they accepted the powers of the president to select new members of the board.

In the previous section it was noted that typically outside directors were chairmen and presidents of companies of equivalent size, top executives of insurance companies and commercial banks, senior partners of investment banking and law firms, and presidents of academic institutions. In addition to the requirement of a prestigious title of a prestigious company or institution for new outside directors, what other criteria are used by presidents in making their selections of new directors?

• The executive vice president and director of a large, widely diversified eastern company said: "It might be worthwhile telling you a little bit about who our outside directors are and how they came into the picture. First is John Brown. The Brown family has been major stockholders, going back well before the 1930s, and the family always had at least one or sometimes two members on the board. John Brown succeeded his father on our board when he died about eight years ago.

"Next is Bill Smith. He is a fellow we acquired by acquisition. He owned a small chemical company which we bought in 1949 and later sold because other product areas turned out to be more promising. I don't know what he does for a full-time job, but he is a very good high-level sales type fellow.

"Next is Gordon Holt. He is an old friend of our president, Walt Stokes. Gordon was a classmate of mine at Wesleyan, and a year after Walt. Also, Gordon and Walt have adjoining summer places in northern Vermont. Gordon is the head of a large family-type enterprise out in Chicago, and I understand he runs it very well.

"The fourth outsider is married to the daughter of the company president who preceded Walt Stokes—a very pleasant sort of guy.

"Next is Jim Parks. Jim is president of Westminster Textiles. Walt got acquainted with him when they were co-chairmen of one year's community fund drive. Later they were on various other civic do's. Walt thought very highly of him and felt his textile experience might be of some help to our products though we are not in textiles.

"Next, Sam Smith is a lawyer from a well-known Philadelphia firm. He and Walt are both trustees of Wesleyan College.

"Jack Hodges is, as you know, president of one of the country's largest banks. Walt has been a director of his bank since time immemorial, and Walt's predecessor also was a director of that bank. Hodges came on our board when he became president of the bank. There has always been a close connection between the bank and our company.

"Next, Joe Marsh is another trustee of Wesleyan. He is head of a small investment firm in Chicago.

"Frank Fox is next. Frank is a senior partner of our principal investment banking firm. We started doing business with them in the late 1940s. The then head of the firm came on our board when that association started. He died, and the spot on our board was transferred over to Frank immediately. Well, that's the list.

"I wouldn't say these men are all cronies of the president. I think that is the wrong word. I think very few can be called close friends of Walt. I think they are people, however, whom he has gotten to know through business associations, and who he has come to feel are well above average in intelligence and ability, and will be good directors—whatever that means. I should point out that the board has never turned Walt down on anything. As a group they are really a nice bunch of guys."

• "Two of the important characteristics required in an outside director," according to one president, "are that the man not be a controversial figure, and not be inclined to stimulate controversy with the management or with the other outside directors. Controversy is not generally looked upon favorably in boards of directors—it is something to be avoided. Controversy is disruptive. The other characteristic is that you want someone who you think is going to be sympathetic to the management—someone who will understand your problems and your shortcomings. Life is too short to have an unsympathetic character on the board."

• "I'm in favor of a congenial board. I don't mean a collection of yes-men, but I do mean I don't want any abrasive s.o.b.'s on the board. I want a board that is really objective, and accepting management at full face value, seeking to support it whenever it sees fit, and only raises issues when it seems important enough."

• "In selecting new outside directors," one president said, "I pick them very much like a trial lawyer goes about the selection of a jury."

• Another comment confirming the importance of selecting sympathetic and friendly directors was, "I'm looking for relatively younger men to get a better age balance than we have, and I want people who would—well, be friendly, if you will."

• "Here in Baltimore there is a relatively small group of leading businessmen who dominate all the principal company boards in the area. They are all fine men, they are public-spirited men, they have high standards and are widely admired. Individually and collectively their names are a credit to the boards they are on. They are friends of friends, and new board vacancies are filled from their ranks and their rosters."

• "Here in New York it's a systems club. There is a group of companies that you can see, and you know them as well as I do, where the chief executive of Company A has B and C and D on his board. They are chief executive officers of B, C, and D, and he is on their boards. They are all members of the Brook Club, the Links Club, or the Union League Club. Everybody is washing everybody else's hands."

• "Don't be surprised or disappointed," one president said, "if you find that most outside board members are known to be non-boat-rockers. What would you do, if you were president? You control the company and you control the board. You want to perpetuate this control. You certainly don't want anyone on your board who even slightly might be a challenge or a question to your tenure, so you pick personal friends with prestige titles and names. With this prestige there is an aura of stability, character, and integrity. You sure as hell are not going to ask Ralph Nader, or Lewis Gilbert, or—what's the name of that woman who is so unpleasant at stockholders' meetings?"

• The retired chairman of a medium-sized company in the midwest stated: "In the companies I know, the outside directors always agree with management. That's why they are there. I have one friend that's just the greatest agreer that ever was, and he is on a dozen boards. I have known other fellows that have been recommended to some of the same companies as directors, but they have never gotten anywhere on the list to become directors. Because if a guy is not a yes man—no sir, he is an independent thinker—then they are dangerous to the tranquility of the board room. Company presidents are afraid of them—every damn one of them."

A few situations were found, however, where presidents with the de facto ownership control and with the power to select outside directors used criteria other than the friendliness discussed above and had a subcommittee of the board as an objective vehicle to recommend names of candidates likely to be helpful without reference to their reputation for passivity or compliance as directors.

• The executive vice president and director of one company stated: "When our company went public about eight years ago, our president completely changed the board. Earlier, the board consisted entirely of insiders, and now the president and I are the only insiders—the other nine are independent, able people. To illustrate the president's thinking, our company, as you know, is concerned with the public's health; our products go into many homes throughout the United States; and the president decided that he needed a senior sort of guy who understood the public-affairs aspects of the industry, and also he needed an able nutritionist. He found both, and they now are great directors. The public affairs gent has essentially veto power on some company policies. The nutritionist, a professor and well-known in academic and professional circles, had never been on a board before, so no one really knew how he might behave—and you know that professors tend to have strong views! He is a distinguished scientist and therefore no intellectual patsy for our president or any other member of management. We know he is not playing games and trying to get along. Recently he objected strongly to a new product proposed for introduction because of questions about its nutritional value. He convinced us in management, and the project was dropped."
• Another president's view, supported by his outside

directors, was: "In most companies you do not have independent-thinking directors. They are generally dominated by management. In this company, though, the independent outside directors control the company, and I am employed by them as president. It is strictly an arm's-length deal. They know, and I know, that if they become disenchanted with my performance as chief executive officer, I go."

MOTIVATIONS OF DIRECTORS TO SERVE

There are three main reasons why busy executives who are presidents of other companies accept directorships but do not participate actively in the management of the company.

Monetary Compensation

One reason for the passivity and the lack of involvement by outside directors is that the relatively modest compensation provides limited incentive to devote time and energy to another company's problems. Meeting fees and retainers have increased in amount during the last several years, but the amounts paid, as one president noted, "are still substantially below what a senior professional management consultant would charge on a per diem basis, and in addition you are asking the director to expose himself to those unknown and uncertain risks of stockholder suits."[1]

• Another observed: "Any board member who is worth his salt is obviously underpaid. For the fees paid, it is not worth the time and effort of an outside director to serve on a board just for the income—there's got to be some other reason."
• "If a board member is going to perform any real function,

---

[1] See NICB, *Corporate Directorship Practices*, Chapter III, "Compensation."

as you and I would like to see him perform, then he is grossly undercompensated. I think it is ridiculous. If you pay $100, $200, or $400 per meeting, you just plain aren't going to get any more value in return. Outside directors are not philanthropists —you can't ask them to contribute their abilities without suitable compensation. If an outside director were doing the responsible job you were talking about, he would be worth his weight in gold."

• "How important," said one president, "is compensation to outside directors? It doesn't mean anything to most chief executives because it is just another thing on top of his 70 percent tax bracket. But were we talking about the lawyer, or the consultant, or the professional director, it would be of some consequence—but not vital, because he could serve on four or five boards and do quite well."

• "The most important fact is that the director can rationalize his not doing very much by the fact that they are not paying him very much. If they were paying him a healthy amount, his conscience would not permit him to do not very much, even though he couldn't keep much of the fee. You may be able to get a president on the board by paying him a small, or a very nominal, amount and not expecting very much of him. But if you pay him, say, $15,000 to $25,000 per year, he will walk up to the job as a director a lot more carefully and with a lot more interest, because he would expect to live up to the $15,000 or $25,000 of value."

• Another president said: "It depends upon what you as president want. If you want your outside board members to be members of value, then you damn well have to pay them, so you have some right to expect them to perform. Then the director has a sense of responsibility. But if you pay him little, how can you expect him to devote more than little time and effort to the job? One of my friends said recently that the low pay of directors was a direct manifestation of the value placed on their contribution by management."

To test the level of appropriate involvement in company operations and to get data on appropriate compensation rates for directors, I asked each person interviewed if out-side directors should be included in company bonus, stock option, and profit-sharing plans. With one exception the responses were negative, and representative comments were:

• "Certainly not. You don't give bonuses and options to people who have absolutely no direct influence on the company's profitability."

• "No. I don't see how you would structure such a plan so that reward would be related to contribution. We have trouble doing it with our vice presidents and division heads. It would be impossible with directors."

• "No. But I can't quite put my finger on why. It seems as though the bonus is an extra incentive for the kind of day-in, day-out effort that managements put into the job, rather than the kind of judgmental decisions you make once a month. It seems to me the bonus awards really ought to go to management. The board is not sufficiently involved in depth so as to be a part of management."

• "I think not. It's a sort of unfair competition with the people who really work at the company and are making the company their career. Option and bonus plans really ought to be maintained only for those people whose principal employment is the company."

• "I've never had that question before. It's not done here, and the reason is that we don't consider outside board members as part of management. To illustrate further, we never send out financial data to directors prior to a board meeting, because that would be disclosing figures to part of the public and not to all of the public. No, board members are not part of management."

• "You can't have outside directors included in the bonus and option plan. Who would be left to objectively administer the program for the key employees?"

The single dissent came from a president who was concerned about the lack of motivation typically found in directors.

• He said: "Now, my four outside directors are a balance of finance, top administrative ability, common sense, and hard-nosed thinkers. Their time is valuable. What worries me is that to keep people like those, we have got to give them an incentive, and the incentive we are trying to work on is stock options. They deserve options in the company just as much as the top employees. We feel that today, with the present tax structure, their time is too valuable to impose upon them to give us a couple, two or three, hours a month unless they are rewarded in proportion to the success of the company in some reasonable way. We want directors who contribute, who direct. We want to attract and keep that kind of director. Also, most outside directors don't want income. They've got that—probably too much. We want to motivate them by having them have the same incentive the key people have to make the company more successful."

Discussions during the field research indicated clearly that top executives regard board fees as low, and with these rates so low they find other explanations for the willingness of executives to serve other companies as directors. The two principal reasons were the opportunity to learn something new in a company or industry different from their own and the prestige value of identification with other enterprises.

Opportunity to Learn

• "I want a little bit of exposure to something different. I don't mind being a director of maybe one company or so, on the outside, so long as it doesn't take any real time. You may pick up a little something—not of a nature that permits you to make two dollars on a stock, but the way other companies are organized, and why."

• "I do it to learn something more about business. For a lot of executives who haven't started on the down curve, who are still aspiring, every board meeting is a chance to learn something. One's own business can make you parochial, the industry can make you parochial. There is a lot more to this world of business than our industry and our company."

• "It's great meeting monthly with a small group of bright guys swapping ideas. This sounds academic, but I mean it when I say that while I don't make any contribution to the company, I go to their board meetings just to listen to interesting and bright people. It enriches my life."

• "Because I want to learn, I want to broaden my contacts and to get inputs from outside the group I live with and work with on a daily basis. I went on the board of a company recently which is strong on consumer marketing—that's an area I want to know more about."

• "I think outside directors, at least the ones I know, think that they will learn a lot—things that may be beneficial to them in their own companies—and I think they do it as I did in the King Company case. The president got hold of me, and talked me into it. It was a personal thing, and I thought I might learn something."

Prestige of the Position

• "There are three elemental human driving forces: sex, hunger, and vanity. Board membership comes under vanity. Serving on a board has nothing to do with remuneration. I've had high level, respectable, and able executives beg to be invited on our board. One said this would be the finest honor that could be bestowed upon him. That is stupid vanity. We play a game of decorations. If I can be on seven boards, I have seven medals and citations, and I'm better than the guy with four. We think this is good in terms of our individual images, in our *Who's Who*, and in our obituaries. The old saying is apparently true: an ounce of image is worth a pound of performance."

• "It's not the money fees. There is no real money in serving as an outside director—it is just money on top of ordinary income. The important thing is the desirability of getting to know better and to be associated with—and in the public eye—well-known people. We like to see our names in a good context. It is good for our morale to be identified with a wise man on the board. And none of us is immune to name dropping. To be able to say, 'Yesterday at the XYZ board meeting, Sam Smith [a well-known president of a well-known large New York bank] said he didn't see much lowering of interest rates for some time to come'—that may not be cash income, but friend, that is income."

• "A lot of companies have limousines and company airplanes to bring directors to and from meetings, and this makes a big impression on some directors. This bothers me philosophically, but it doesn't bother me personally, because (a) I'm not on any boards like that—I was, and I resigned from several boards of companies just for those reasons; and (b) I haven't got those things in my own company, so it isn't a personal problem for me."

• "I like the idea of sort of being ranked with a lot of first-class men and getting to know them. It's human and it's perfectly natural. You get to sit next to them, and then chat with men of stature, and you are sort of classified as a first-class citizen. And that's why you build stature on your boards."

• "Prestige is important, but that is wearing a little thin these days when directors are being sued by stockholders. When the attraction of being an outside director of, say, one of the top 500 companies wanes, it's going to be increasingly people who are serving on boards for some kind of self-interest—an investment banker, or a commercial banker, or a lawyer, or a customer, or a supplier—people with interests not necessarily coincident with the interests of the stockholders."

CONCLUSIONS

Most of the outside directors of large and medium-sized companies interviewed were chairmen or presidents of other companies of equal size, top executives of commercial banks, or leading partners of distinguished investment banking and law firms. Most of them believed that the prestige names and titles of outside directors were critically important, principally to enhance the public image of the company—as it was colorfully put by one, as "attractive ornaments on the corporate Christmas tree."

I found that among company presidents this preoccupation with titles and prestige names as critical requirements for outside directors meant neglecting the possible contribution to company operations of able but less well-known people with less prestige.

Chief executives who serve other companies as directors are exceedingly busy men, and their carefully budgeted time schedules cannot allow substantial diversions. Devoting 12 to 18 hours a year to the board problems of other companies does not permit any perceptive and meaningful understanding of company problems. And to assume that company presidents—busy company presidents—will spend the time to do the homework essential to understanding company problems is asking more than should be reasonably expected. Their own stockholders would be short-changed if the president's time and energy were diverted to the problems of another company. The issue is clear: How much time can you realistically expect an extremely busy company president to spend on another company's problems?

The use—the exploitation—of prestigious company titles of prestigious companies to enhance the public image of a company is hardly the purpose for which boards were required by the early and current laws on corporations—"The company shall be managed by a board of directors consisting of at least three persons." And to state to a stockholder public that eight well-known and respected company presidents are serving the company as outside directors implies that these directors are spending appropriate amounts of time in the stockholders' interest. This is misleading. Presidents of other companies typically cannot, and do not, do this.

It was found that the powers of control in most instances rested with the president, and he accordingly had the power to determine the membership of the board of directors. In the exercise of this power most presidents looked for candidates who, in addition to having prestige, were believed to be capable of working as members of the board team in the constructive interest of the company. Also, when the presidents identified their choice for election to a directorship, they usually corroborated their choice with existing members of the board and ostensibly gained their approval.

Almost every discussion of criteria used in the selection of outside directors stressed descriptive words and phrases such as "friendly," "sympathetic with management," "non-controversial," "congenial," and "our kind of people." There were few examples of outside directors who by reputation were known as boat-rockers or wave-makers. "Life is too short," said one experienced member of management.

It should be expected that presidents, aware of their powers of control and sensitive to the personal values and benefits of their positions as heads of business organizations, would be unlikely to nominate members to their boards who might in any way jeopardize their tenure at the top of their companies. Presidents, it was found, generally liked their jobs, and tended to avoid any possible or potential threat to their positions.

A few situations were found, however, in which presidents insisted on an arm's-length relationship with their boards, and recognized and acknowledged one of the classical roles of the board, namely, to select and if necessary to replace the president. These examples were rare.

It should be noted again that when the president's powers of control are counterbalanced by substantial stock representation on the board, he does not have the full de facto powers of ownership, and he does not typically have complete control over the selection of new directors. The amounts of influence exercised by other holders of power vary tremendously, and their exercise of power cannot be generally forecast. Some holders of power choose not to use it; others utilize every ounce of the value of this position; and there are many variations between these extremes.

Outside directors in general are not involved actively in the company they serve for the financial income, which is nominal at best. The monetary compensation nets a very small increment to their real income, particularly in view of the still modest, though increasing, sums paid to outside directors. They are willing to devote some time to the companies they serve, but little more than attendance at one-and-a-half-hour meetings, and they rationalize their lack of interest in giving more time to this by noting that their compensation is lower than senior professional management consultants charge on a per diem basis.

Directors accept board memberships, not for the income, but for the opportunity to learn how other companies operate and for the prestige value derived from an identification with other impressive names. These motivational forces encourage busy executives to accept board membership, but not to devote more than casual amounts of time to the fulfillment of any significant standards of performance.

This does not mean that corporate outside directors are not men of integrity, character, and responsibility. Indeed they are. But with the demands of their own positions of primary responsibility, and with the nominal nature of the dollar income from fees and retainers, busy company presidents are not motivated to spend much more than a minimum amount of time on other companies' board matters. And the minimum time usually is equal to the hours devoted to monthly or quarterly board meetings.

CHAPTER VI

Inside Directors

Sнould inside full-time employees other than the chairman of the board and the president serve on their company's board of directors?

Of the 456 manufacturing companies covered by the 1966 NICB report on directors:

Only 27 manufacturing companies (6% of those reporting) have a perfectly balanced board in terms of outside and inside directors, having an equal number of each. However, some companies do not find a board composed of both inside and outside directors necessary or even desirable. Six out of the 456 manufacturing companies studied (slightly over 1%) have boards composed entirely of company executives while, at the other extreme, one company has no employees on its board and five other firms have only one employee director.

Outside directors constitute a majority in 63% of the boards of manufacturing companies studied in 1966, indicating that the steady trend toward a predominance of outside directors has continued.[1] This trend has been observed since The Conference

---

[1] The 63 percent figure is overstated, since members on boards who are retired and former company officers are regarded as outside directors rather than inside directors. The 456 manufacturing companies covered by the NICB study had 2,859 outside directors, of whom 342 were retired or former company officers—roughly 12 percent of the total. Indeed except for commercial, investment, and private bankers, there were more retired and former company officers serving as directors than any other occupation. See NICB, *Corporate Directorship Practices*, Table 6, p. 15.

Whether retired and former company officers are regarded as insiders or outsiders is moot. My own preference is to regard them as insiders, because of their knowledge of operating details of the company and the industry, and their organizational loyalties developed over the years.

Board's initial study of directorship practices in 1938 showed an even split between boards having a majority of outsiders and those having a majority of employee directors. Outside directors constituted a majority in about 54% of the manufacturing companies in 1953 and 57% in 1958. In 1961, nonemployee directors were in the majority in 61% of the companies surveyed.

Employee directors occupy 42% of the total number of seats on the boards of the manufacturing companies, down 2% from the 1961 figure. Whether employees constitute a minority on a particular board seems unrelated to company size, since the percentage of companies having a minority of employee directors show no distinctive pattern when firms are ranked by assets. For example, the greatest percentage of companies (72%) with a minority of employee directors appears in the third largest asset category, while the next highest percentage (71%) occurs in the next to the smallest asset group.[2]

Most of the executives interviewed during my field research for the present study stated firm convictions that boards of directors should include insiders in addition to presidents and chairmen. Conclusions varied as to the appropriate proportion of insiders and outsiders, and as to what was meant by the phrase "a balance of insiders and outsiders." But almost all participants stated that a significant percentage of insiders should serve on company boards. The broad rationale for this conclusion was stated as, "You ought to have several inside operating and functional executives on the board when the company is a large, diversified operation. The reason is that if questions arise with regard to marketing, finance, or the problems of an operating division or subsidiary or what have you, there is an executive at the board table to whom you can turn and say, 'All right, now here's a question. You answer it.' That is his field of endeavor. It's not possible for the president or the

---

[2] NICB, *Corporate Directorship Practices*, p. 6.

chairman of a large-sized company or even of a medium-sized company to be knowledgeable on all the important details of company operations."

MORALE AND PRESTIGE

The most common combination of reasons for having insiders on boards was expressed in terms of individual and organizational morale and prestige.

• One president said: "Take any company. As it grows larger and becomes big—I don't care what industry it is in—it has a tendency to become bureaucratic. Then you find your key people more and more wanting prestige, if you will. The individual wants to say, 'I am not only an executive vice president of the company—I am also a director.' It has nothing to do with his contribution at board meetings. He wouldn't dare say anything that disagreed with his boss, so therefore he can't make any contribution to a board discussion. It's strictly a matter of pride and prestige."

• "Inviting insiders to serve on the board is just one more way of providing a distinguishing symbol—like a key to the washroom. There is an important morale factor involved in it."

• "In order to attract and hold a top man, you have to put him on the board. It's an honor."

• "I just think to myself, as a human being, that if I were just sitting in a board meeting, in the back row, as a sort of second-class citizen, and I were thinking about my life, and I am a guy in my fifties, I'd say, 'Hell, what am I doing here in the back row?' As boss man of this company, I think the corporation in its total compensation package for its top guys has to include membership on the board—the place of plenary power. 'Mr. Vice President, you have full voice as a director, and you have the professional stature of a director.' I think that means something—not only to the vice president but also to his subordinates. The very dignity and feeling that you are on a par as a director with all the other directors, inside and outside, is great for his morale."

• "A directorship for the inside executive is a status symbol, important within and outside the organization. The individual, in terms of the outside, is judged. When you talk about being a member of the board, that is important. Are his peers on the outside saying, 'By God, he is a director—he is listed and has his picture in the Annual Report'? Just among his peers and colleagues on the outside, I think this is a tremendously important symbol."

• "There is a psychological advantage in having the top insiders feel that they were part of the board's final decisions, and that these decisions were arrived at jointly by the outsiders and the insiders. The insiders were involved, and were there in roles which were much more than just flunkies."

• One strong dissent to the morale factor of board membership was expressed: "To the idea that having insiders on the board gives a spirit of morale to the entire management organization because they say to themselves 'Someday I can be on the board,' I say, 'So what?'"

EXECUTIVE EDUCATION IN TOP MANAGEMENT

The second principal reason given for having insiders on the board was described as educating the inside executives on the management process at the board level, and getting key insiders involved in the process.

• One president said: "The process of management is to get overall the right decisions made with regard to the operations of the company. That decision-making process has to be a composite one, and on balance it's better to have the best brains from the operating levels participating all the way up in this decision-making process. In our own company we are highly divisionalized, and I believe that our outside directors can do a better job as a result of having direct contact with, and direct inputs from, the three executive vice presidents who are on the board. I think it makes a difference whether the insiders feel they are part of the process, part of the club. And I think it is highly educational for them. It can be said of course that they could attend board meetings as guests and not as members. But I think that there is an important difference of degree, and that their involvement in the management process as directors is important. It isn't the same when you are sort of sitting on the sidelines."

• "The presence of insiders on the board gives substance to the meaning of multiple management. We are a large corporation, and I don't think that the management's position should be reflected in one man's personality or one man's view. Now, whether it takes three, or five, or more to do this, I won't argue the point. We have three active insiders on the board at the present time, and we have three other people who are really ex-employees. These two groups of insiders and former insiders bridge the gap between the management and the outside directors better than anyone else."

• "I think an important advantage of having insiders on the board is that they feel freer to speak than if they were just sitting at the meeting table without the right to speak. Secondly, I think it involves them by being on the board in terms of the company's overall prospects. I think it is helpful to say, 'We will give one of our operating divisions a look at the board meeting, and I am asking you as a director of the company, and as general manager of another operating division, to view this not just in terms of your own division, but in terms of the overall company. You, as a director of the company, have got to take a company point of view, which is greater than your own division point of view.' So I think to that extent it gives the insiders a broader responsibility—which, in the top level of the company, is good."

• "I would be the first to admit that we have some insiders on the board who make absolutely no contribution in the meeting, or any contribution to total company functions except those of departments reporting to them. This I hope will be corrected as time goes by. But we have one inside director who heads a major division where we have half a billion dollars invested, who is a broad-gauge entrepreneur and a thoughtful and persuasive salesman. Over the years, as a board member, he has learned a good bit about our other operating divisions, which are in much different product fields. With this education on the total business, he does make a contribution in our board meetings as well as outside the board meetings. The fact is that he is thinking about our whole business—not just his part of it. Sometimes his ideas aren't worth a damn. But he is thinking beyond the boundaries of his product lines, and that is more than you can say about a lot of inside directors."

• "All key men in the organization who are regarded as candidates to succeed to the position of chief executive officer within the next few years ought to be on the board in order to have an understanding of what the total company picture is, and what board relations are like."

EVALUATION BY OUTSIDE DIRECTORS

A third reason cited for having insiders on the board was to enable outside directors to become acquainted with, and to be in a position to evaluate, inside executives' capabilities to succeed the present chief executive officer.

• One president said: "The theory is, of course, that the outside board members, if called upon to act in the crisis situation of the unexpected death of the president, ought to have calibrated the potential of insiders to take over the top job. A good way for outsiders to get acquainted with key insiders is to work with them as fellow board members. Outsiders can observe how well the various insiders know the facts about their functions or divisions, how effectively they make reports and presentations to the board, and how well they handle themselves in the environment of the board room. I think that the outside board members should know as much as they can about the capabilities, character, temperament, and what not of key insiders. If I get hit by a truck tomorrow, my successor undoubtedly would be picked from the insiders now on the board."

• "When insiders operate as peers with outside directors, the association encourages conversation and discussion. Through this exposure the outsiders can tell what makes the various insiders tick—what their strengths and weaknesses are, and which of them seems to be qualified to be the next president."

• "When presentations or reports are made to the board by inside directors, you have a pretty good opportunity to judge them and to gauge their capacities for the presidency. Without this exposure the board never really knows anyone below the top job. I think key insiders should be on the board, if only to enable outside directors to get to know them."

• "After our monthly board meetings we always have a luncheon for board members, inside and outside. This informal affair permits outside directors to arrange to sit and chat with the insiders whose operations interest them. In the absence of expressed individual seating preferences, we try to plan a rotation of insiders sitting with different outsiders each month. The luncheon table is really a great place to talk about company problems and company opportunities."

Other presidents, however, did not regard the board level exposure of insiders to outsiders as having merit.

• One said: "When a division manager makes a presentation to the board, even if he is a member of the board, he knows that he is being evaluated, being judged, by the outsiders. Accordingly he sure as hell will be on his best behavior. He will do his best to be cogent, and try to give all the evidence of an orderly mind, and that sort of thing. Actually it's an artificial, synthetic exposure of key people, and impressions created can be as wrong as they can be. If the outside board members base their judgments largely on the impressions made at board meetings, they will reward glibness and poise, and penalize wisdom and maturity."

• "In my experience outside board members' reaction to reports by inside directors is based almost entirely on the type of presentation a fellow makes. I remember down at a chemical company one time, the board was really strong on appraising key people by the reports they made. Everybody knew it. One poor fellow collapsed just before his presentation. He was so nerved up and keyed up that he just literally collapsed. And it wasn't because of any shortcomings in the content of his report —he knew he was going to be judged on what he did, and how well he handled himself on his feet. This is a ridiculous and false criterion."

Board Membership as Help in Recruitment

Some presidents explain the presence of inside executives on the board as a condition of their employment.

• "If you are trying to recruit a key man, say a VP of finance or a VP of research and development, one of the attractions can be membership on the board—especially if he's not on the board of his present employer. Sometimes board membership is more important to the man than an enormous increase in salary. And if he is a first-class fellow, we usually say, 'All right, let's have him on the board.' I've had some terribly good people turn me down just because we felt we couldn't have any more insiders on the board."

• The president of one company, who was considering two possible job offers in companies three times the size of his present one, said: "I would have no questions about leaving here as president and taking on a job as executive vice president in either of the two opportunities. But both offers would be much less attractive—in fact I wouldn't consider them—if membership on the board was not included. I wouldn't go with either company unless I expected to be top man in the near future, and you don't do that by starting way down in the wilderness of the organization."

• "A problem I am having these days, with high surtax rates on income, and with stock options having virtually no appeal because of the new tax rules on holding the stock, is keeping and motivating my key people. They are good, and they are approached constantly by headhunters who hold out bright vistas of employment by their clients. Some employers offer all sorts of perquisites and long-term contracts. The one thing I try to make available to hold a key man who is comtemplating leaving is something to enhance his stature, and that is membership on the board. This is another way of saying to him—but more importantly of showing him—that he is really an important man on the management team."

REASONS FOR NOT HAVING INSIDERS ON BOARD

Other presidents expressed the view that inside executives other than the president and the chairman should not serve on their companies' boards.

• "It is hard to believe," said one president, "that an inside officer as a member of the board is responsible for evaluating the management of a company which he, among other board members, has delegated to the chief executive officer for whom he works. That is the dilemma, and that is where the conflict begins."

• "The vice president inside-director type is in a very precarious position at a board meeting. He just can't say anything in disagreement with his boss, so what he usually does is sit quietly and wait until he is called upon to speak. He's got to walk such a tightrope! He must be sure that nothing is said or implied which would be offensive to the senior management of the company."

• "If you watch what happens at board meetings, you will observe that any questions are asked by outside directors and never by insiders. And it's a little bit like a tennis match—if a questioning outside director is at one end of the board table, and the president is at the other end, the question and response results in all eyes moving in unison to whoever is speaking."

• "Insiders don't ask questions or raise issues at board meetings because their points of view and contributions have all been expressed at meetings of management prior to the board meeting. All the insiders have been through the monthly performance review. Rarely—no, *never*—does the head of one operating group raise a question at the board meeting concerning the performance of another operating group. He would not do that at a board meeting. If he had a question or an observation, he would raise it with me privately. If a question occurred to him at the board meeting, he would raise it with me after the board meeting. This happens quite often. After a meeting, for example, our international VP might say, 'I don't understand why the products manager was concerned about further devaluation in Italy. Surely he is covered on that risk. If not, he should be.' I would explain what the international VP had in mind, and it could be that the point made was a valid one. But you've got to remember that nobody likes to gore the other fellow's eye, especially when the act gets seen or heard by other members of the top management, including the board."

• An executive vice president and inside director said: "We have a sort of rule around here—we've even formalized it in a sense. Now, we fight like cats at the management meetings. But if any of our key inside people on the board feels strongly opposed to something the president is asking the board to approve—and again, this doesn't happen very often—rather than go to the meeting and vote for it contrary to his judgment, he just doesn't go to that particular board meeting. This is sort of a screwy idea, but that's the way it's done here."

• "We have two insiders on the board now—the chairman and myself—and we've got all the insiders that we have any intention of having. If you have more insiders, you have a continual problem of deciding who is on, and who is not on, and why. If you have a complete minimum of insiders, such as two, and that number has been pre-set as a precedent so that nobody thinks much about it, you don't have a whole lot of birds wondering why one person is, and another person is not, on the board. It's much harder, too, when you have a company vice-president on the board. Once an internal guy gets elected to the board, he becomes more difficult to cope with, from the standpoint of the chief executive. This has nothing to do with the board room process, but just in the daily administration of the company. This cookie now becomes in his board capacity on an equal status with the president, because in the final analysis they are both just fellow members of the board. It is not that the vice president will challenge the president at a board meeting, but there is a definite change in the relationship between the president and the vice president. I think it is much better to maintain a working relationship based on the president and vice president status rather than complicate it by having vice presidents as members of the board."

Another reason given for not having insiders on the board was the embarrassment resulting from a request that the insider resign from the board if the change seemed appropriate.

• One president said: "Once you put an insider on the board, you cannot ask him to leave the board so long as he continues as an employee of the company. You can't do it from a morale point of view. You can build all the rationales you want to, such as, 'It would be in the best interests of the company if you would give up your seat on the board to the head of a recently acquired large subsidiary.' But this won't sell. It would demoralize not only those you asked to step down, but also all the people in the departments in which they work. Sure, it can be done—but only with a terrible risk that the morale of the organization will go to hell."

• "I am a director of a very large industrial products manufacturing company, where the president is an old friend and law school classmate. As he restructured and hopefully strengthened the organization about five years ago, he went outside and hired half a dozen key people, most of whom came aboard as vice presidents—three as vice presidents and members of the board as well. The president believed sincerely, when these three particular men were hired, that they would be candidates for the presidency. But it just hasn't turned out that way. For this purpose, we got the wrong guys. They are very good in their respective jobs, but everyone now agrees with the president that his successor is not to be found on the inside. The result is that we really are stuck with the three insiders on the board, unless we want to lose them as employees by asking them to leave the board."

To avoid the problems resulting from putting "the wrong insiders" on boards, some presidents adopted the policy of rotating key executives on the board for two-year terms. More insiders were exposed to the benefits of board-level discussions, and their departure from the board after two years caused no loss of face or embarrassment to the men leaving the board. Other companies follow essentially the same process by electing three insiders as permanent members of the board, and using seven other board seats as rotating memberships for insiders.

Other reasons for not having insiders on the board were expressed as follows:

• "We considered putting the division managers of our six divisions on the board, but concluded that that would be just too much domination by insiders. I don't want it. More importantly, I don't want the man who is running our radio stations to be concerned about our motel business. I think that is a mistake. He has enough problems of his own without (a) being confused by another division's problems, or (b) being asked to think about somebody else's problems for which he has no line responsibility. We do arrange meetings of the top managers from time to time, so that by reference they might find a lead or an idea or a contact for the others. But it's only on that basis. I sure wouldn't want these managers ever to think that as inside directors, they have responsibility for the whole company. I don't like that idea at all."

• "I don't need to have insiders on the board to have access to their thinking. Any time I want their judgment all I have to do is to walk down the hallway and ask them. Having them on the board gets just too parochial, too personal. We end up talking to ourselves. This is sort of intellectual incest. What I want are the ideas of outsiders, and every time you put an insider on the board you are depriving yourself of one more input from an outsider. A friend of mine is a very strong executive. He started his business in the back of an undertaking parlor, and today his company is large and one of the leaders in its industry and listed on the New York Stock Exchange. It is typical of a lot of companies dominated by a powerful and able entrepreneur. I am on his board, but most of the other directors are over-aged insiders, some retired, and some still active in the management. These insiders are products of a narrow business environment, isolated from any business other than the one which has employed them for many years, and they haven't had a new idea in about the same amount of time. They contribute nothing to the board meetings. They are there only because the president feels some sort of loyalty to old friends, some of whom have been with him from the start."

• "A board consisting largely of insiders results in an awful lot of in-breeding, and at least in theory outside directors prevent that and give you different points of view from what you are exposed to anyway in the day-to-day operations of the business."

BALANCE OF INSIDERS AND OUTSIDERS

Almost all the executives interviewed stated that some sort of mix of insiders and outsiders on the board was desirable. Judgments as to the appropriate proportions of the mix varied among the executives, but with few exceptions there was general agreement that a "good" board included outsiders and some insiders in addition to the president and the chairman. Reasons given for preferred mixes were quite imprecise, and were typically based or turned on executive judgments rather than on logic.[3]

- One said: "I think it is a mistake to have all outsiders except for the chairman and the president. Board matters need the points of view of both sides. For no very good reasons, I like to have half and half."
- "I like what we have now: eight insiders and six outsiders."
- "I know that insiders' only function at a board meeting is to report on their areas of the business, and I know that they speak only when spoken to. But I also know that when insiders are sitting at the board table they contribute a sort of insulation for me against what might be some embarrassing questions from outside directors. A commonly observed courtesy practiced at all self-respecting boards is not to embarrass the president in the presence of his subordinates. I don't know how many insiders are necessary to provide that insulating immunity from discerning questions, but I want as many as are required!"
- "Unless the president has absolute and complete control of the corporation, it is a mistake to have a majority of outsiders on the board of directors. If you get a lot of guys from the outside, even though you pick them, you lay yourself open to a takeover deal. To avoid this, I think the board should be stacked predominantly with insiders. In my company, for example, we have nineteen directors—four outsiders and fifteen insiders. Now if you've got a family-situation company where the family has absolute control, and there is no chance of a takeover, then I think it's probably all right to have more outsiders than insiders on the board. For instance, Kelly [president of a medium-sized manufacturing company]. He personally controls the corporation. He owns enough stock, his family owns enough stock—something like 39 percent, or something like that —so there's no possible way for any outsider to get control. So

---

[3] The latest NICB study on directorship practices reports that the trend to a predominance of outside directors in the manufacturing companies included in their research continued, and that in 1966 outside directors constituted a majority in 63 percent of the boards studied.

in that case he has more outsiders on the board than insiders.

"A lot of people say that the main reason for having control of the board in the hands of inside members of the management is to assure the continuity of management. And the reason they don't put a large number of outsiders on the board is that they want to perpetuate their own management of the company, their own chauffeurs and cars, their own airplanes, their salaries and options, and all the rest of the stuff people talk about. Well, of course they do! And the stockholders can do one of two things: one, sell their stock—and if enough people sell the stock will go down, and the options, the salaries, and everything else will be affected; or two, the stockholders can band together and elect a new board. The stockholders, you know, do have the right to change the board if they want to."

CONCLUSIONS

During the last twenty years there appears to be a steady trend in increasing the proportion of outside directors in large and medium-sized companies. All of those interviewed during the field research indicated that the ideal board of directors had some sort of balance of insiders and outsiders. The appropriate balance varied among the interviewees—some favoring more outsiders than insiders, and others preferring control in numbers by the insiders. Only a few of the executives and directors questioned on the issue of balance on the board expressed the concept that there should be no insiders on the board other than the chairman and the president.

Those who favored insiders on the board observed that by being on the board insiders were present and available to answer any questions which might arise concerning their respective areas of responsibility. Board membership, it was noted, gave prestige to the insider, rewarded his service to the company, served as a source of nontaxable intangible compensation, and contributed to the building of not only the insider's morale but also the morale of the subordinates in his organization.

The educational values of board membership—values to the insiders and values to the outsiders—were repeatedly given as a reason for having insiders on the board. It was believed to be good for insiders to gain an understanding of the management process at the board level, to provide them with management points of view beyond that of the function or the division for which they were responsible. In addition, outside board members, through association with insiders at board meetings, would have useful exposure to candidates who might succeed the president—they could gauge how well the subordinate seemed to know his operations, and how well he was able to communicate as he made reports and presentations to the board.

The few interviewees who were opposed to insiders on the board stated that no inside board member can very well evaluate the management of which he is a key member, or express judgments inconsistent with or in qualification of those expressed by the president. It was suggested that once an insider was elected to the board, it was difficult to remove him if organizational circumstances should make the change desirable.

Whether insiders other than the chairman and the president should be on the board essentially turns on the president's concept of the functions of the board of directors. If the president perceives the board as a relatively meaningless level of the management structure or at most as an element in the corporate image, any number of insiders can be on the board. But if the president perceives the board to:

1. Provide advice and counsel—insiders do not have to be on the board in order to advise the president;

2. Serve as some sort of discipline—how does an insider on the board serve as a discipline on himself?

3. Be available in the event of a crisis—can insiders objectively conclude that their bosses' performance is so unsatisfactory that he should be replaced?

4. Determine objectives, strategies, and major policies—inside officer directors can recommend objectives and strategies, but should those who recommend also approve?

5. Ask discerning questions—can an inside officer director ask discerning questions at board meetings without jeopardy to his working relationships with the president?

6. Evaluate the president—how does an officer director with aspirations of continued employment evaluate the president except in favorable terms?

How can any insiders, other than the chairman and president, be on boards of directors?

I believe that the seemingly plausible reasons given for having insiders on boards of directors are essentially fallacious and specious. The objectives of the reasons cited for having insiders on boards could be accomplished through other means. I conclude that presidents who insist on having insiders on boards do not regard the role of boards to be much more than using the statutory requirements of boards to serve the ends of employee morale, and to dampen rather than to encourage questions, discussion, and involvement by outside directors. I doubt that the historical or present intent of the corporation law envisaged such a limited role for boards of directors.

CHAPTER VII

Investment Bankers as Directors

O NE of the principal sources of outside directors for large and medium-sized companies is the investment banking firm and its partners. The early rationale was that their presence was required on the boards of companies for which the firm had underwritten new issues of securities in order to represent the shareholders who had purchased these securities. In addition, investment bankers as professionals in the financial world were regarded as primary and supplementary resources for advice on top management financial problems faced at the board level.

During the last decade, however, investment bankers, company presidents, representatives of governmental legislative and regulatory bodies, students of business, and others have questioned whether officers of investment banking firms should serve on boards of directors of publicly held enterprises. This issue was discussed with all of those interviewed during the field research.

INVESTMENT BANKERS AS SOURCES OF ADVICE

Some of the top executives interviewed believe that members of investment banking firms *should* serve on boards of directors. They suggested that investment bankers are a valuable source of advice for company managements, not only on financial problems but also on other functional and general concerns of the presidents of the company served.

- One stated: "Investment bankers have an enormous fund of knowledge about how other companies face and solve their problems. In the course of their work they get exposed to a variety of companies and industries, and they can bring to board discussions a much broader background of experience than, say, the president of a limited product line company. A mature investment banker typically has had a career of dealing with top management problems, and his wisdom can be of enormous help to a president and other members of the board."

- "The investment banker on our board is one of the real old pro's of Wall Street. He is in his early sixties and is as alert as his colleagues who are twenty years younger. He brings to our discussions insights gained from his experiences of many other companies; and his sharing of the lessons learned in other situations helps us, I am sure, to avoid some of the same pitfalls. An investment banker by the nature of his business is more than a source of financial advice. He is more like what some people have called a professional director."

- "I don't think a man should be disqualified from serving on boards because he is an investment banker. The right investment banker can be most helpful. I believe candidates for board membership should be looked at as individuals with breadth and ability who can contribute. If I find such a man, I want him on my board, and I don't really care if he is an investment banker or not."

- "The appraisal by a director who is an investment banker of how the financial community will evaluate what you are contemplating doing is very helpful. He is able to translate to us how what we propose will be regarded by the Street."

- "We have two investment bankers on our board. I think two is better than one, because the members of the investment banking fraternity can see that we are not a closed shop. Also we've found that the services of both firms were exceedingly helpful in our recent tender offer for the Rowley Company.

They worked out the details of the proposal to other members of the board. We needed the help of outside financial people, and I doubt that we could have done it at all, much less as well, if we depended on our own inside financial people to explain the intricacies."

• "Any company of any size needs the services of an investment banker. It is one of those services that a company really has to have if it is going to do its job of growth. If you are going to have those services, you are going to have to motivate the guy who provides the services needed, and one way is to have him on your board. The nature of the relationship is such that it pretty much has to be an ongoing one, and board membership assures this. When we review financing alternatives we need the investment bankers' advice—for example, on what kinds of restrictions large insurance companies have insisted on recently, what are the points an insurance company lending money to us will give on, and what are the points they are absolutely adamant on. Also the investment bankers' advice is important in the area of acquisitions. They know many imaginative ways of structuring deals. That is a part of their business. We in management are novices relative to their involvement in hundreds of deals.

"Also, having a partner of a well-known investment banking firm on your board declares to the world that the company has good sponsorship. If your company is identified with a little known and perhaps not highly regarded investment firm, a lot of people would say, 'That must be a second-rate security.' Sponsorship can mean many things to investors. The message can be conveyed that the investment banker is saying in effect, 'We vouch for this company's management. They are honest, capable, and we are willing to go to bat for them in raising any additional money they need. Or we will go to bat for them overseas. Or we will go to bat for them in lots of ways.' So sponsorship by a reputable and well-known firm can be very important indeed. And sponsorship by a good firm is most effectively communicated to investors by having a partner of the firm on the board. Your company has been labeled—a little bit like the Good Housekeeping Seal of Approval."

Assistance Without Board Membership

Others interviewed acknowledged that investment bankers could be of enormous assistance in resolving top management problems, but suggested that the professional advice of an investment banker can be obtained without having him on the company's board.

• "Take Bill Jones, who just came on our board. He was the head of a large investment banking firm which has the policy that their officers are not allowed to serve as directors of companies until they are within—I think it's one or two years of retirement. When they get within one or two years of retirement, then they start accepting invitations to be on boards. Bill is, as I said earlier, one of the truly outstanding figures on Wall Street in the sense that unlike many of these investment banking people, you will always know that you are getting an answer that is just what Bill thinks is the right answer for your problem. He doesn't think of it in terms of his firm, or—you know, scratching somebody's back. He is honest and frank. If he doesn't agree with you, he tells you so. We have turned to Bill Jones for the last twenty-five years for his advice and help. He has just been of tremendous help to us in anything that relates to our financing—I mean how we raise money, where are we going to look for money, what to pay for it, who to use. On all these questions he's just invaluable. Now, we were getting the same sort of advice from Bill before he was elected a director. With him as a director we are not getting any more or any less help. As for the advice he gives, I don't think the quantity, or the quality of it, or the nature of it, has changed since he became a director. So far as advice is concerned, it doesn't make any difference whether he is on the board or not."

• An investment banker said: "I have been a director of three large listed companies for at least fifteen years, and during that time, and without undue modesty, I have been the chief source of outside financial advice for these companies. I am sure I have made substantial contributions and suggestions to the managements, and I am sure the managements would agree. I am equally sure, however, that these same substantial contributions and suggestions could have been made without my being on the boards of directors. The board membership formalizes the relationship between our firm and the companies, and makes it easier to maintain continuous working relationships. Without board membership there is a little bit more burden on their managements, and a little more burden on me, as an investment banker, to maintain the professional business relationship. I know it can be done because I have a considerable number of other corporate clients whose boards I am not on. I know as much about their operations and problems as I do about the companies where I am a director. If a law or regulation required that investment bankers resign from the boards of directors of publicly held companies because of the conflict of interest issue, I would welcome the rule. I am not too sure about our professional competitors though. Some of them would scream—they have had locks on some companies for fifty years through representation on the boards. Any jeopardy to those locks would be resisted vigorously."

• The president of one company suggested that professional people who provide services to the enterprise should not serve on boards. "I think generally speaking that it is a mistake to have on your board representatives of service organizations such as investment bankers, commercial bankers, outside legal counsel, management consultants, and so forth. The specialized knowledge and wisdom of these people can be bought and paid for. It is not necessary or desirable to have them on your board of directors. If you have such persons on your board, you discourage imaginative entrepreneurs in that same field from approaching you with good ideas, because any business is going to go to his competitor who is already on the board. I have always felt that you shouldn't have on boards people whose services you buy, because they are also in the business of serving other clients in other parts of their own business."

Interviews during the research revealed two main cluster points bearing on the issue of investment bankers on boards of directors: (1) with access to inside information as a director, an investment banker is usually involved in a direct conflict of interest and has access to data not available to other investment bankers; (2) an investment banker on a board identifies the company with that specific banking firm and restricts the management's freedom of action in relation to other banking firms.

CONFLICTS OF INTEREST

The Views of Two Investment Bankers

• A partner of one firm described the conflict of interest issue: "If an investment banking firm has an investment counseling service, provides brokerage service, controls or manages a mutual fund, then they are involved in giving investment advice on securities to clients. The advice may be to buy, sell, or hold. If partners of the firm serve as outside directors of listed or unlisted companies, it is inevitable that investment advice will include securities of companies for which firm partners serve as directors. The conflict of interest in this situation is unavoidable. It's in the nature of the business. Efforts are made to maintain the separateness of the investment firm's research department from other parts of the firm. But as you might expect, these separations, by the nature of things, are really artificial. Are there slips between the various activities of a firm?—Of course there are!

"Another example of conflict is found when investment banking partners serve as directors of companies with securities sold on the over-the-counter market. Usually when a firm manages the underwriting of a new issue, it agrees to make a market in the stock issued—that is, it agrees to perform essentially the role of a specialist on the floor of the New York Stock Exchange.

The over-the-counter department of the investment banking firm is a separate profit center, and the manager of the department, as well as the partners of the firm, want the over-the-counter department to be profitable. The over-the-counter department makes money not only through commissions, but also by serving as principal taking a long or short position on the issue. If the over-the-counter department is long on a particular security, it has an interest in the price of the stock going up. If the over-the-counter department is in a short position, it has an interest in the price going down. In this situation there are two kinds of conflict: (1) if the o-t-c department is long on a particular stock, it would like to have its sales organization recommend the stock or have a favorable report from the research department, so the shares can be sold at a higher price; and (2) the decision to go long or short is made easier by having access to information as to what is going on in the company. Now, if a partner of the investment banking firm is on the board of the o-t-c company, there can be an enormous amount of pressure on the partner-director to communicate with the o-t-c department.

"The conflict of interest is clear, and real. I was involved in such an incident recently. At a board meeting of a company whose stock we brought out, and where I have served as a director since the new issue, we voted a stock split and the stock went up sharply on news of the split. The day after the directors' meeting I caught hell from the manager of the o-t-c department for not letting him know earlier about a possible stock split, because when the news was released to the public, he was caught short several thousand shares. As he pointed out to me, rather firmly and eloquently, I cost our firm thousands of dollars. So you see the reality of the pressures.

"Some people think there is some sort of mystique about investment banking, but it just isn't all that complex. Basically, we generate income by having investment ideas. If we know more than our competitors, if we have information that they do not have, we have something worth dollars to our clients and therefore to ourselves. We make money on the information we have. Information is critical to our success and profits. Since a director has, or is presumed to have, access to more information than the usual investing public, he is motivated as a partner to promote the interest of his firm. Communications between the partner-director and others in the firm interested in company information need not be explicit or reduced to writing in a memorandum. If I stop by the research department and say, 'You ought to send someone up to the XYZ Company—there are some mighty interesting things going on there,' this message is about all they need. Last December one of my partners asked whether he should sell his personal holdings in an o-t-c company where I am director. I refused to tell him. All I said was, 'Well, I'm not going to sell any of mine.'

"It must be remembered that investment bankers, whatever their function in the firm, are after all people, and you simply can't stop people from talking."

• A partner of another investment banking firm suggested that while a conflict of interest exists for the partner-director, internal procedures and practices on the part of the firm can preclude legitimate question or criticism. "There is, however, a valid question of conflict of interest in the case of any director. This relates to the possession of inside information, and the potential use of such information, directly or indirectly, most especially in connection with stock prices. While this danger is by no means confined to outside directors or investment bankers —you will recall that in recent widely publicized legal cases the principal culprits were officers of the company, and some of them quite middle-level officers at that—there is no doubt that outside directors have a particular responsibility; and there is equally no doubt that investment bankers, by the nature of their business, are surrounded by particular opportunities for conflict, and have therefore quite properly received a particular amount of attention from those who have examined this problem.

"I think there are no universal conclusions. There are those who feel that the solution would be to prohibit investment bankers from serving on corporate boards in any event. While the enactment of such prohibitions would be welcomed by some investment bankers—every conscientious investment banker I know considers that much of the time, effort, and energy which go into his directorships in comparison to the amount of business which can ever be done with one company could much more profitably be directed to other endeavors—I am by no means certain in my own mind that this would be a wise type of prohibition in the broader context of American business. It would deny to corporate boards many men who are among the most qualified in the country to serve on boards. It would also deny to corporations many insights, both into the state of the economy and into the state of the financial markets, and in generalized terms into the progress and problems of other companies and businesses relevant to the corporation as seen through the eyes of experienced and knowledgeable men dealing daily with these matters. In this regard it seems to me that such a prohibition would significantly narrow the range of experience available to a corporation for its board. Furthermore, such thinking tends to be progressive: if investment bankers are prohibited from serving, it seems likely to me that questions would soon be raised about the propriety of commercial bankers serving, perhaps lawyers, and even professional consultants, and indeed anyone who might be in a position, theoretically, to benefit from the possession of inside information.

"The fact is, none of us is immune from such opportunity. Corporate officers themselves are actually in the most sensitive position, since they not only have inside information, but can directly and immediately control and alter it.

"My own firm has wrestled with this problem for at least twenty years—long before, I am happy to say, it became a matter of general concern either to the SEC, the stock exchanges, or others. We have never found a perfect answer, but we have evolved a set of practices which at least satisfy us that our methods and activities are beyond the reach of any legitimate question or criticism. We have accomplished this for many years past by adopting and rigidly enforcing a few simple and basic internal firm policies:

"First, we discourage any partner or associate from assuming a directorship, and we permit it only in cases where our relationship with the company is particularly close, or the company is particularly anxious that we serve, and where we feel there is a positive contribution which we can offer to the company by serving.

"Secondly, we insist upon strict compartmentalization. We do not permit any director to speak with any other partners (or any others within the firm) on matters relating to the company of which he is a director, except on matters legitimately relating to the company's business, or in response to legitimate questions within the bounds of response set down by the company itself.

"We do not permit the research department or any other person in our firm ever to issue a written report on any company in which any member of the firm holds a directorship, even though the analyst writing the report might do so solely on the basis of his own knowledge gained by his own research. We feel that the implication involved that 'inside information' might have been available to him is unacceptable.

"The firm never trades for its own account in the securities of any company in which we hold a directorship, except at times and under circumstances fully known to and approved by the company. We do generally try to hold a position in the securities of any such company, which position we consider as frozen. With regard to customer accounts in the house, many of which naturally have holdings in such companies from time to time—often partially because members of our firm are on the board, and our customers seem to give credence to this fact—we take every possible step to insure that no such account is the beneficiary of any inside or advance information, either as regards other accounts which we handle or as regards the general public.

"We continually require all our personnel who are directors of any corporation to read and initial every significant court case or other regulation relating to the duties, responsibilities, and liabilities of directors, in order not only to keep them constantly aware of the current legal situation, but also to insure that these things don't get forgotten with the passage of time.

"Finally, in the setting of fees for any services which we may render, and in deciding for which services we will or will not charge, we follow the practice toward a company in which we hold a directorship of being lower and more conservative—often significantly—than we would be in dealing with a regular corporate client, precisely to prevent the possibility of any legitimate question ever being raised with regard to such matters.

"While these internal regulations are stricter than those followed by any other investment banking house known to me, the fact that they have been in force and enforced for many years has been a source of reassurance to our partnership that we have done everything humanly possible to prevent becoming involved in problems such as have beset others.

"There are certainly firms—I am satisfied that they do not include any of the major firms—which as a matter of policy will get by with whatever the traffic will bear. Much more often there are individuals within firms, even the best, who are either dishonest or more often careless. Perhaps some day this fact will cause a regulatory agency to throw the baby out with the bath. I personally hope not, for I feel that this baby is a vigorous and important part of the American corporate structure.

"In the last analysis, the only protection any of us have—within our own firms and corporations—against such matters is the integrity and competence of those we associate with. I would not have as a partner anyone whose integrity I doubted. You would not want to see anyone serving as a director or officer whose integrity you doubted. We can of course be wrong in our judgments, but I doubt if it will happen very often if we avoid falling into carelessness."

A Director's Point of View

• An outside director of several financial institutions and manufacturing companies described the conflict of interest issue: "I am not a lawyer, so what I describe as common sense conflicts may or may not be in violation of any laws. Some investment bankers see several areas of conflict. One is that investment bankers typically want to be directors of companies they take public, in order to represent the shareholders' interests—and in particular to represent their clients' interests. Yet if they become directors, and if they continue to advise their clients, inevitably they will face a conflict where they know something about the company, where the shareholders would want to take action, and this would affect the price of the stock. Say they, as directors, find out something bad. In their role of trying to protect their shareholders' interest—which is the only reason they went there in the first place—they may want to recommend a sell, or somehow may want to get out of the stock. Yet this may very well be at the most sensitive time for the company. So the investment-banker director, presumably a fiduciary for all shareholders, is really representing a small and specific group of shareholders, and the conflict is there.

"Another kind of conflict involves the established large company and an investment-banker director. Directors are presumed to know what is going on in their respective companies, or at least to have access to sources of information which enable them to know what is going on. In some recent situations investment bankers resigned from all boards to avoid the suspicion that their investment advice to clients was based on inside information and not on research. In one case the investment firm changed a company's earnings estimate and recommended that the stock be sold. One of its partners was a director of the company involved. The question is whether the earnings estimate was changed as the result of a shrewd and perceptive analysis of the company and its environment, or for other reasons. In any event, the investment-banker director just can't win. There was no way that firm could recommend a sale of that particular stock without coming under a cloud of suspicion. So one thing or the other has got to go: either the banker stops being on the board, or the banking firm stops following the stock. If they stop following the stock, why are they on the board?

"And in my judgment the conflicts are going to get worse. The economics of the industry are forcing firms to become multi-dimensional. The marketing economies make it economically desirable for a firm to offer a mutual fund, a counseling business, a pension trust, information service, and lots of other things. The economics that force them to do all these things in

one organization increases the conflicts until they are unbeliev-
able."

Some Views of Presidents

• A top executive said: "I think a particular problem with
having investment bankers on your board is that it puts them in
a kind of conflict-of-interest role, because they are always passing on the value of your stock. Now if you have a very frank
kind of discussion at a board meeting, where does that leave
them? The investment banker board member has obligations to
his partners, and if he hears or sees something we are having
a problem with, he advises his partners responsible for the
investment portfolios, who then may decide to sell our stock.
Also other investment advisers on the Street who are not represented on the board are likely to think that here is a man who
knows something that they don't. Sometimes that is not the way
it happens. Sometimes the portfolio manager doesn't agree with
his partner's advice. But nevertheless, the suspicion is there in
the minds of other people who are not on the board. Directors
have an obligation to represent *all* the shareholders instead of
certain ones. As soon as you have an investment banker, you
put yourself in a position where one group of shareholders
might be favored at the expense of other shareholders. I think
investment bankers should not be on board. We have one now,
but that situation will be changed shortly."
• "There is no doubt," said one president, "that investment
bankers can make very great contributions to a company's top
management thinking. In their business they analyze one company after another, and they know something about how other
companies are managed. Having studied things, and having
done their homework throughout their business careers, they
have a sixth sense as to whether things are good or bad. But the
conflict of interest is always there. I think it is a very delicate
situation—so delicate that they should not serve on boards of
directors. But so far as being able to make a contribution is
concerned, I think that they are extremely valuable people."

• "The problem of having an investment banker on your board is that he is immediately involved in a direct conflict of interest. The danger is very real. He is subject to all of the risks of hindsight. If his firm has a man who recommends a position on the company stock, even without inside information, the partner-director will never be believed that he is not involved. He may be innocent, but will look guilty as hell. Everyone will say, 'There must have been communication,' and nobody will believe that there was not."

• One president stated: "We have an investment banker on our board. He was on the board before I came in from the outside as president. Several months ago he called me and suggested that I evaluate the possibility of acquiring the Jay Company. I studied all the data and concluded that the Jay Company was not a growing company, and was in a relatively stagnant industry. While I was studying the Jay Company the investment banker conducted a sales campaign with the other outside directors, especially the company's outside legal counsel. The possible acquisition of the Jay Company was raised at our next board meeting, and I, as president, was the only board member who was opposed to the acquisition. It was disclosed at the board meeting that the investment banker had negotiated for a commission to be paid if the acquisition went through. When I objected that this was inappropriate for a board member, the board as a whole agreed to leave the amount of the fee to be negotiated by our company counsel and the investment banker. A few days later I was advised by the legal counsel that $250,000 seemed an appropriate amount for the size of the deal to be consummated.

"At our next monthly board meeting the legal counsel and the investment banker brought in a contract they had negotiated for the purchase of the Jay Company. Again the matter was discussed, and again I voiced my opposition. I was outvoted, and I indicated that I would sign the agreement in a sense under duress. And I did. We then released the news to the press, whereupon I received a telephone call from a large stockholder who had read the terms of the deal in the newspaper and concluded that I had lost my mind. The large stockholder warned

me that he was opposed to the acquisition, and would do everything he could to block it. He was able to enlist the support of
enough stockholders to block the deal.

"I am completely convinced that it would have been a bad
deal, that the investment-banker director's primary interest was
not our stockholders and the company, but rather the $250,000
fee, and that it was almost impossible for our investment banker
to be completely objective as a director of our company. The
wounds of that battle still remain, and I doubt that they will
ever be completely healed."

• "The nature of the business makes it impossible for an
investment banker to be completely objective on the financial
dealings of a company served. When a situation comes up that
forces an investment-banker director to choose between what's
good for his firm or what's good for our company his first loyalty
is obvious. And for the life of me I can't figure out why it has
taken us so long to figure that out. No investment banker should
be on any board of a company with which his firm has any
dealings."

• "Investment bankers are not dumb. They are all aware of
the built-in conflict. Many of them today would like to resign,
especially in the light of what has happened in some companies.
The real reason they don't resign is that they know that their
competitors will rush in and try to get the business away from
them. Their problem will be solved only when all investment
bankers agree to resign from boards, or when some law is
passed, or when the risks related to their being on boards
clearly outweigh the rewards to them."

Other Views of Presidents

Some of those interviewed, however, believed that the
essential conflict-of-interest issue was not a disqualifying factor for an otherwise qualified and desirable investment
banking firm partner.

• "I think the ethics of business and of directors is far better
than it is given credit for. In my experience the number of

times when there has been any violation of high standards of conduct through the availability of inside information has been nil. Sure, you see once in a while a big deal is reported in the press, but when you think of the thousands and thousands of potential violations, the occasional and I would say rare instance of using inside information is nothing. The only value of the widely publicized stories of a violation is that it reminds people that when you wear two hats, you'd better be pretty damn careful of how you wear them. I don't see why the fact that an investment banker advises people about investments damns him from all boards. In the first place that is heresy, and in the second place you are impugning the integrity of all investment bankers without evidence that they do in fact use the information. Also, who in the world can sit in a board meeting and know whether the company's stock is going to go up an eighth or down an eighth—based on what goes on in the typical board meeting!"

• "With today's SEC requirements for the timely and full disclosure by company managements of significant events which might affect security prices, the to-do about conflict of interest for investment bankers is academic. Sure, years ago before the disclosure requirements there might have been a problem—but not any more."

• "I don't think the problem of investment bankers having access to inside information creates any conflict of interest. I don't think that that is a real danger with reputable firms. I have seen absolutely no evidence of that happening in our company, and I have been around here for over 25 years. I am confident of the integrity of the investment banker on our board. I would have no objection, however, if the industry practice or specific legislation prohibited investment bankers from sitting on corporate boards. But I'd like to point out that we are experiencing more difficulty all the time in finding competent people to sit on our boards where there is no conflict of interest."

• "It is not fair to blame directors for leaks of inside information. There are an awful lot of other people who get the information earlier than the directors, or at the same time as the directors. And with our corporate headquarters here in the Wall Street area, you know, probably everybody here in our organization has a friend who works for a bank, or a securities house, or somebody interested in what we are doing. Having an investment banker on the board makes it easier, I suppose, to get the information accurately. But I don't think that that is any great disadvantage to anyone."

• "Having an investment banker on the board legitimatizes the communication by management on company operations to a considerable extent, as compared to communications with someone in the investment community who is not on the board. The same information in the same hands can be protected properly and for the good of the company, or it can be utilized improperly and to the disadvantage of the stockholders."

MANAGEMENT RESTRICTED TO ONE INVESTMENT BANKING SOURCE

The second issue cited by those interviewed in having or not having investment bankers on the board was that the company could become identified with one investment banking house, thus restricting the management to the services of the firm represented on the board.

• One president stated: "Having a senior partner of an investment banking firm on our board is notice to the world that we are his captive client. Of course this is the main reason investment bankers want to be on so many boards. They think of board memberships as a very good way of assuring that the business of the company goes only to them. It's a sort of Operation Stakeout. It tags the company as belonging to one particular firm."

• "A director of a large New York company described the restrictive effect of identification with one firm: "Several years ago the president of the Doane Company concluded that the company's product line had limited potential for growth, and that a growth plan for the acquisition of other companies in diversified fields was necessary. He discussed the concept at several board meetings, and asked all the board members, especially a partner of an investment firm to assist in identifying product areas and interesting companies which met the management's acquisition criteria. The company's investment banking firm had been represented on the board for over 15 years. Now, two years passed with absolutely no recommendation from that firm. The president, knowing that I had some experience in acquisitions, asked me to discuss the problems and opportunities with the company's investment banking firm, and others, and to help in getting some sort of an acquisition program moving.

"I arranged to see the partner who served on the board and his colleagues, and after a long discussion concluded that this investment banking firm was not particularly skilled or active in providing professional services in the acquisition field. Their inability to help the Doane Company during the previous two years was attributable directly to this lack of skill and this inactivity. As I left the group discussion, our investment-banker director asked what else I planned to do, and when I told him I was going around the corner to see my friends in the XYZ investment banking firm, I noticed that he visibly winced. When I arrived at the XYZ Company offices, the receptionist asked me to call the president of the Doane Company immediately—it was urgent. I did, and he asked that I not have any conversations with partners of XYZ, and suggested that I come uptown and have lunch with him right away.

"At lunch the president reported that the investment banker on our board had called him as soon as I left his office and said, 'For God's sake, don't let Mr. A. talk to anyone at XYZ. That would be a terrible black eye for us. We have been your investment bankers for years, and if anyone from the company talked with another firm it would suggest that you are not satisfied with the job we are doing for you.'

"The president complied with the director's request, and the company's only Wall Street resource on acquisition ideas continues to be that one firm. It is interesting that the Doane Company has not really been able to use any other firm, yet our investment banking friend has never, ever, even up to today, come up with one constructive idea in the field of acquisitions. That is just not their game."

• "If you've got an investment banker on your board, you're sort of a little bit tied in with him, and I prefer not to have one on our board. An investment banker on the board restricts one's freedom of action—I mean you might or might not want to use his firm in some transaction, and if he is on the board he thinks he is entitled to that business."

• "We don't have any investment bankers on our board. Some have asked to come on, but we turn them down even though we have lots of good friends in the investment banking business. We love them, and I think they are smart guys, great guys. But we have never wanted to feel any sense of obligation to one firm. The investment banking community thinks that there is an implied relationship to do business with them as soon as they get on the board. They feel that in the acquisition field, in the whole area of financing, they have a proprietary position. It's a club kind of thing. The investment bankers fight like hell to preserve their clients, and bring all the pressure they can to keep you from moving out of their orbit.

"Let me illustrate the advantages of not being tied to one or identified with one Wall Street house. Three or four years ago we repurchased some of our stock, and we got the K Company to do it. They were the right people to do it—they have a whole network of offices around the country, and they did it efficiently. On the other hand we have done long-term financing three times through the M Company. K is less good at that, and M is great in setting up bond syndicates and selling bonds. M seems to be able to get better terms than K, because for years they have been calling on the little insurance companies and the little pension funds. We have a couple of long-term financial agreements with commercial banks, and these we handle directly ourselves. Now, if a partner for the K Company or the M Company were on our board, he would want to be involved exclusively. If we did not use them, their feelings would be hurt. We think that management should use the best financial services available to do the particular job to be done. If you are tied to one investment banking firm, you are restricted to their services, even though they may not be particularly qualified to provide those services.

"Not only does an investment banker on your board restrict your options, but also he wants to be involved—and always for a fee—when you don't need or want him to be involved. For example, if you go to an insurance company for money, the investment banker on your board wants to take you over there by the hand and be the intermediary. I don't mind the fees they charge—we pay lots of fees—but it's just that I don't think we need them. Maybe if a company is reasonably small and the management is reasonably unsophisticated, with limited experience in exposure to the Wall Street community, then an investment banker can be helpful in dealing with an insurance company or a bank. But even here, you don't have to have the investment banker on your board to get these kinds of professional financial advice."

• The restrictive effects of an investment banker on the board was confirmed by a senior partner of an investment banking firm who stated: "If we identify three companies as equally logical candidates to acquire a company which we represent, and two of the three have representatives from our investment banking competitors on their board, we will always go to the company without another firm's representative on the board. On going to this company we have a better chance of picking up a new investment banking client, we may avoid having to split a fee, and we often have a better chance of selling management our idea since we don't have to buck the N.I.H. feelings of a board member competitor. In most cases when we find a strong competitor on a board, we don't even approach the management, because we know they have a lock on that company's business."

• "Having an investment banker on the board binds us to that firm—it binds us to do all of our business with them, and that's not good. Recently we issued some convertible debentures, and the conversion rates and the terms of the deal were all made basically by our investment-banker director. I had no basis for knowing whether we could have done better with a different banker. I don't really know whether his advice was in the interests of our company or in the interests of his firm.

"I don't care whether you are talking about monopolies or oligopolies—when there is no competition, the costs are just plain going to be higher. I can't think of one single good reason why we shouldn't have competition when we get involved in major financing."

• "We brought out some debentures a few years back and we had no investment bankers on the board, so the field was wide open. We shopped the issue and got a broad spectrum of rates from various firms. We took what we thought was the best, and today we've got some 4.6 percent money on our books, and I wish we had a lot more of it."

• "If you had a multimillion dollar deal to be done, this could be financed in a whole variety of ways. And if you go to several imaginative highly-skilled financial pro's, each one's individual recommendations will be quite different. As a president with financial problems of this magnitude, I must get the expertise of more than one financial pro. If you eliminate this competition you just know you're going to pay more."

INVESTMENT BANKERS ON BOARDS NOT RESTRICTIVE TO MANAGEMENT

While most of those interviewed believed that having a partner of an investment banking firm on the board limits the management to the services of that one firm, a few top executives took exception.

• "That whole myth that an investment banker on your board limits you to that firm is nonsense. We have a well-known investment banker on our board, and he is absolutely no constraint on what I do with other firms. I tell him what I am doing. Recently I told him I planned to use the Y investment banking firm for a bond issue, and his response was, 'Sure. They have the people to do that job. We don't.' "

• "There has been a marked change during the last two

years with regard to the limiting effects of having an investment banker on our board. It used to be that he, by his presence on the board, was *your* banker. But today sophisticated professional investment bankers know that firms vary as to capacities and abilities. Some are great for distribution in the United States, and are weak in Europe. And if the firm represented on your board is weak in Europe, the director is not likely to object to your using someone else who is strong there. The investment banking business is getting more complicated, and it's perfectly natural for different firms to have varying degrees of expertise in different areas and functions."

• "We have an investment banker on our board, and up until recently have done all of our business with his firm, the X Company. Last year we had a $60 million financing for a new plant. Before we went to a second firm, the X Company sent a man out, and he just couldn't get what we needed. So I went to another Wall Street firm that sort of specializes in that kind of financing. I caught hell from our investment banking director. He absolutely believes that his firm could have done the job better, and that we belong to him. He is most unhappy because I felt that the interests of the stockholders would be served better by the other house, and that I do not consider that we are limited to his firm alone. It was a little bloody, but that old Wall Street myth—that because an investment banker is on a board he owns all the business—is pure bunk. Maybe that's the way it used to be, but times have changed."

CONCLUSIONS

Investment bankers represent one of the larger sources of outside directors on boards of large and medium-sized companies. The investment banker, by the nature of his business, is exposed to a wide variety of companies, industries, geographical regions, countries, and corporate policies and practices—financial and otherwise. This exposure contributes to his breadth of experience and wisdom as a businessman. Most of the executives and directors interviewed stated that because of their wide experience investment bankers make enormous and important contributions to corporate management thinking and to discussions at the board level. Investment-banker directors were described as great pollenizers. They brought to the company served as a director knowledge gained in other situations—knowledge and perceptions not likely to be otherwise available to the company top management. Many interviewees stated that in addition to having breadth of experience, partners of leading investment firms were bright people, with the capacity to understand complex top management problems, even though the intricacies of the particular industry or company were not fully comprehended. Many of those interviewed shared the conviction expressed by one: "Candidates for board membership should be looked at as individuals, and investment bankers typically have wide experience very valuable to board discussion and resolution of major corporate problems. Investment bankers can make valuable contributions at the board level."

It was found, however, that from the point of view of top management there are two important considerations that suggest that representatives of investment firms should not serve as directors of business corporations: (1) conflict of interest, and (2) restriction of company managements to the professional services of only one firm.

An investment banking firm, in addition to its underwriting function and other corporate financing services, typically does investment counseling, employs brokers, and controls or advises mutual funds. The performance of these functions creates an inevitable internal conflict of interest for the partner of an investment banking firm who serves as a director of a business corporation. Unless the firm refuses to deal in, or to advise the purchase or sale of, the securities of companies where partners are directors, the conflict of interest for the partner-director is inevitable. And the dilemma for the partner-director is: Do I represent the interests of the stockholders in the company served as a director, or the interests of the firm of which I am a partner? Resolution of this dilemma by stating that he serves both at the same time—what is good for the corporation is good for the investment banking firm—cannot be accepted in good conscience as valid in all cases; and neither can the creation of rules and regulations with regard to communications between partner-directors and other interested, profit-centered, responsible officers of the investment firm. Investment bankers may be people with wide experience and exposure to business practice, and generally bright and perceptive. But they are people. It is unreasonable to expect that people will behave in a manner inconsistent with, or inimical to, their best interests as they perceived them.

Most of the company presidents interviewed stated that partners of investment banking firms typically were experienced and able contributors to the solution of management problems at the board-of-directors level. But, they added, the motivation of investment bankers to serve as directors of business corporations was primarily to assure that the investment banking relationship with the company would be maintained and protected. Interviews with investment bankers confirmed that their main reason for being willing to devote time and energy to being a director of a company was to keep the investment banking business of the corporate client, and to get exposure to other directors in order to generate new banking business. They see board membership primarily as a "business-getting device." They would not serve as directors if the investment banking business was "shopped around the Street."

It was found also that presidents without investment bankers on their boards were approached from time to time by members of investment banking firms suggesting that they be invited to serve so that a closer working relationship through board membership could be established. One investment banker asked to be elected to a company's board, giving the reason that he could do a better job for the company. The president responded with the question: "In what ways could you do a better job than we are now paying you for doing?" This remains an unanswered question.

The presence on the board of a partner of an investment firm in most cases is notice to the world, including other investment bankers, that a client-banking relationship has been established, and that the company's business is limited to that firm. The result is that often other investment firms with services, skills, acquisition opportunities, and information of value to the company will approach other more likely customers who don't have an already identified bank relationship.

Those who believe in the values of the competitive system will recognize that in those situations where a vendor knows he has an exclusive relationship with a buyer, the vendor is in a position to engage in practices which could not be enjoyed under conditions of free and open competition. The benefits of monopoly in business not operating in the public interest such as public utilities have not yet been demonstrated. So it is with investment bankers and their clients. Research interviews did not suggest that identification with, and commitment to, one investment banker was desirable from the company's point of view. Rather the reverse was found to be true.

It was found also that investment banking firms, like any service organization, have professional skills of varying degrees in the various fields in which they operate. Some firms are especially skilled and strong in marketing bonds, others in marketing stocks or convertibles; others are distinguished by their operations and staffs with expertise in international financial markets. For a company president to be limited to the particular abilities and skills of one firm represented by a partner on the board deprives the management of superior abilities and skills to be found in other investment firms. If a company needs help, say, in acquisitions, the investment banking firm represented on the board may be weak in this area. Not to be able to go to other and more qualified firms deprives the management and the stockholders of better professional services.

Based on the evidence accumulated through the field interviews, I conclude that representatives of investment banks should not serve as members of corporate boards of directors.

*   *   *   *   *

On the question of investment bankers serving on boards of directors, the company presidents interviewed typically expressed firm pro and con judgments, but when the issue of whether commercial bankers, especially those representing banks with trust departments, should serve on boards interviewees generally showed little interest in discussing the question. They stated, "Commercial bankers are different," "The commercial banker-director probably represents the company's lead bank but most large and medium-sized companies deal with many other banks so management is not limited to that one bank," and "The commercial bank's trust department is run as a completely separate operation and a possible conflict of interest is more theoretical than real and completely different from the conflict that an investment banker has." With the lack of interest in discussing commercial bankers as board members relatively few data were gathered in the interview process—certainly incomplete and inadequate for any conclusions.

But if one of the principal reasons for not having investment bankers on boards is that they have a conflict of interest resulting from access to inside information, it would appear that commercial bankers representing banks with trust departments share the same disqualifying conflict of interest.

CHAPTER VIII

Directors in the Family Company

A FAMILY company,[1] for the purposes of this study, is one in which family members and their associates exercise control over a corporation. Some of those interviewed during the field research referred to such companies as "closely held corporations." The distinctive factor of a family company is the power to exercise control by one or a few members of a family.

The characteristic difficulties and unique and underlying psychological problems of family businesses have been described by Professor Harry Levinson:

The difficulties of the family business begin with the founder. Usually he is an entrepreneur, for whom the business has at least three important meanings.

1. The entrepreneur characteristically has unresolved conflicts with his father, research evidence indicates. He is therefore uncomfortable when being supervised, and starts his own business both to outdo his father and to escape the authority and rivalry of more powerful figures.

2. An entrepreneur's business is simultaneously his "baby" and his "mistress." Those who work with him and for him are characteristically his instruments in the process of shaping the organization.

If any among them aspires to be other than a device for the

---

[1] Since the field research for my doctoral dissertation in 1946 and 1947, I have continued to be interested in boards of directors of family companies. This chapter updates the findings published in 1948.

founder—that is, if he wants to acquire power himself—he is soon likely to find himself on the outside looking in. This is the reason why so many organizations decline when their founders age or die.

3. For the entrepreneur, the business is essentially an extension of himself, a medium for his personal gratification and achievement above all. And if he is concerned about what happens to his business after he passes on, that concern usually takes the form of thinking of the kind of monument he will leave behind.

The fundamental psychological conflict in family businesses is rivalry, compounded by feelings of guilt, when more than one family member is involved. The rivalry may be felt by the founder—even though no relatives are in the business—when he unconsciously senses (justifiably or not) that subordinates are threatening to remove him from his center of power.[2]

STOCK OWNERSHIP AND THE POWERS OF CONTROL

In small, newly organized family companies, members of a family typically own all of the stock, and exercise de jure powers of ownership and control of the company assets. As the company grows, its stock is distributed beyond the members of the family, sometimes as a result of a public issue, sometimes as a result of stock issued with the acquisition of other companies, and sometimes as a result of stockholding members of the family giving or selling shares to others outside the family. As the stock becomes more widely held, the de jure powers of ownership and control inherent in the ownership of 50 percent or more of the company stock by family members shifts to de facto powers of ownership and control. Some situations were found in which representatives of company-founding families exercised de facto con-

2 Harry Levinson, "Conflicts That Plague Family Businesses," *Harvard Business Review*, March-April 1971, pp. 90–91.

trol of large corporations while owning only a small percent of the voting stock. Other situations were found in which the family control of a company ceased when its ownership became less than 50 percent, and the de facto powers of control moved into the hands of other stockholders. The new exercisers of de facto control might be members of another family, and the company would still be regarded as a family company with only the name of the family changed. Or the new exerciser of power might be a president who took over the de facto powers of control.

There were many examples of shifts of control by one family to control by members of another family; to control by new outside stockholders and combinations of stockholders; and to control by a president who assumed the de facto powers of control when large numbers of stockholders were unorganized and essentially unorganizable. It was not the purpose of this project to study the process and reasons by which these shifts of control took place; rather it was the purpose of the project to study what directors in fact *do*, in family corporations with different centers of control.

Directors as a Source of Advice and Counsel

It was found that in most family corporations—in corporations in which de jure or de facto powers of control were exercised with stock ownership ranging from 2 percent to 100 percent—members of the board of directors served as sources of advice and counsel to the family controlling the enterprise. In some family-controlled companies a member of the family was president, and in others a nonfamily professional manager was designated by the family to serve as company president. In the latter situation board members served as sources of advice to the nonfamily president, but their primary role, and their primary responsibility, was to provide advice and counsel to members of the family who exercised control over the company. Whether the president was a member of the family controlling the enterprise or a professional nonfamily member selected to manage the family company, the outside director, it was found, served primarily in most cases as a source of advice and counsel to the family exercising control.

• To illustrate. In a family company the chairman of the board who had started the enterprise forty years earlier selected as president and chief executive officer a key member of the marketing staff who was not a member of the family, and who did not own any appreciable number of shares of stock. The chairman who, with members of his immediate family, owned 15 percent of the voting stock, withdrew from the day-to-day management functions but maintained a periodic and continuous interest in the company, principally through monthly meetings of the directors. To strengthen his sources of advice, he invited six outsiders and the president to serve as directors of the company.

The chairman described his concept of the function of the board of directors. "In a family-controlled enterprise such as ours, even though today we own only 15 percent of the stock, the allegiance of the board of directors must be completely to the family. The only exception would be if there was fraud or dishonesty, or something like that—then there is some sort of responsibility to the nonfamily stockholders. But since the family put the directors on the board in the first place, the primary responsibility of the directors is to advise the family. The directors should study the company operations, be aware of the benchmarks by which to measure how the president is doing, and develop some ideas as to what is good and what is bad policy.

"The board members should advise the family and help them make the decisions. If the family gets too far out of line, then they should tell the family, 'Well, I'm going to vote against you, because I think you are wrong.' Or they should say, 'I won't serve on your board, because I don't like what you are doing.'

"If it gets down to a vote, then the family factor dominates and determines the decision, no matter what a majority of the board members conclude. If it were something really important, and the outside board members couldn't convince me that I was wrong, then the outside directors would just have to resign. I want their advice and counsel, but make no mistake—if it gets down to my judgment versus the composite judgment of outside directors, my judgment and my decisions will prevail. I control this company. I created it forty years ago, and I will make the final important decisions. The outside directors were invited to serve on the board with the hope that they would teach us something we don't know. That is the reason why they are there. I think the outside board members should have a balance of widely diversified functions and experiences—men who have contact with the outside world. We have an engineer, a financial man from Wall Street, a marketing specialist with ingenuity and awareness of what's going on in the marketplace, and three others who can bring mature and wise judgments to the party. I need and want this advice, but it must always be remembered that the role of the board is to advise me, as head of the family that controls the company."

• Another family company chairman said: "My father-in-law started this business. I came in shortly after graduating from college, when I married his daughter. Her father was one of the midwest pioneers in the fine, expensive, high-end-of-the-line furniture industry, who saw the signs on the wall many years ago and moved the production facilities to the South. During the last two years some interesting and not very good things have been happening to this part of the furniture industry in the United States. We had two directors who were pushing me to move into other related and unrelated businesses through acquisition. They pointed out, both inside and outside our board meetings, that our segment of the industry was not a growing segment, that as a publicly owned company there was a responsibility on management to enhance the stockholders' investment, and that if we limited ourselves to that part of the industry in which my father-in-law pioneered, we would be in deep trouble. Then they said that if present circumstances continued, the company inevitably was headed for years of a slow decline in sales and earnings.

"I talked this problem over with my wife, and we decided the company should stick to its last. Our part of the furniture business really created the company, and we concluded that we should not forsake it now in troubled times. It was good enough for Father—it should be good enough for us. Before our last board meeting I went to New York, asked the two outside board members to lunch, and requested that they resign from the board. They did resign immediately. They failed to realize that they were essentially advisers to me and members of the family, and they failed to realize the tradition of the company and the family identification with it. You just don't change, or attempt to change, a business formula which has been mighty good to the family for many, many years."

• An outside director of a family company stated: "I have been a director of the Kay Company for three years. The company is controlled by the Smith family. They owned 100 percent of it until about five years ago, when they went public. The Smiths today own about 18 percent of the voting stock. The father is chairman, and the president is a long-time employee who is not a member of the family. Last year the old man really became disenchanted with the president. Sales and profits, though about equal to the previous years and well above the competition, were less than planned and in the budget. The chairman decided that the president should be fired, and the night before one of our monthly board meetings the chairman told me, 'Tomorrow I will ask the president to resign, and I want you to vote in support of that action. I control the company, and I have decided that the president must go. And I want you to agree.' I said, 'Aren't you putting that a little bluntly?' And the chairman responded, 'Yes.'—Well, there you are. There is no question in my mind that the most I can do is to advise the chairman and the members of his family. Sure, I could have resigned. But what purpose is served by that? The chairman would just have added somebody else to replace me—someone who would fulfill the role as adviser."

DIRECTORS AS ARBITRATORS

Another function served by directors of family corporations was found to be that of arbitrator or conciliator. Not infrequently two or more members of a family, vying for dominant power in a company, find differences of judgment which they are unable to negotiate to a satisfactory conclusion. It was found that nonfamily directors were added to the board with the hope that they, exercising outside objective judgments, would be able to reconcile differences among family members.

• The president of a family company said: "I have been the head of this company since I graduated from the Harvard Business School. My father created and built the business and now is what could be euphemistically called quasi-retired. His title is chairman of the board, and theoretically he is not involved in company operations. When I came in, we agreed that his salary would remain the same, that he would keep his company car, office, and secretary, and that he and Mother would spend the winters in Florida. The board of directors consisted of Dad, Mother, the company lawyer, and me. We never met formally as a board even for annual meetings—the lawyer took care of whatever legal requirements there were.

"The first year the folks went south for the winter, and I ran the company. This all sounds great. But the old man got restless and began looking around Florida for sources of supply for some of our purchased items. He agreed to put $100,000 of company funds into some sort of a commercial fish deal, and in February he flew back home with an idea for a new health pill which he insisted we go into. He got the description of the ingredients from some character in Florida, hired a packaging consultant in Miami to design the label of the package, and to create some ads and direct mail pieces. This was totally outside our existing business, which was industrial chemicals. We knew nothing about consumer items, and in my judgment we should not spend any time or any more money on such a crazy venture. Dad was adamant, but I finally got him to agree to get the outside advice of one of my classmates who worked for a bank in Chicago. He spent a day with us, and at the end of our discussion we all agreed to stick to our present business and not go into the consumer end. Dad went back to Florida, but before leaving suggested we add the classmate-banker to our board of directors. The banker agreed, and we initiated quarterly all-day meetings of the board.

"During the next few years Dad continued to meddle in plant operations when he was in town. He would walk through the factory and make suggestions to the plant manager and other supervisors. He would ask for special reports from the financial department, and he would thumb through the mail on my desk. I found it very hard to get him to stop. He would listen to what I said, but somehow not hear what I said. He would nod his head, apparently agree, and then go right out and do the same thing over again. My classmate and now company director became my confidant, and he was enormously helpful, although not entirely successful, in getting the old man to recognize that he had to leave the management to me. The classmate had long discussions with my mother and father, got them both to see that what they wanted most was for me to succeed in running the company, and that the minor involvements by Dad—minor as separate incidents, but major in terms of my control of the organization—jeopardized the goal they wanted most. It took some time, but the consultant was most useful in helping to 'transish' the old man out of operations and into retirement."

• The classmate-director, a vice president of his bank at the time of our interview, described his experiences with this family enterprise. "This was the typical family corporation problem, with the father being succeeded by a son as president. We see this classic example almost every day among our customers at the bank. The father owns and controls the company, but wants to take it easy by having his son as successor. The son perceives this as a great opportunity, and both father and son have good, charitable, generous, and considerate thoughts about each other and the company. But in almost every case I know about, conflicts arise between father and son and get intensified and compounded by the blood relationship. And the poor sons, knowing that what they have represents the results of what the fathers have enabled them to have, develop deep feelings of guilt when the inevitable evil thoughts towards the fathers arise. These are emotional messes.

"In this case I remember the many long discussions I had with the father and mother in the living room of their apartment. After the father had been rebuffed on one of his daffy ideas by his son, the father would be furious. I listened to his tirade for two hours, one night. The father was emotional and said things about his son that he would never say about an executive of the company who was not a member of the family. The son was ungrateful, unappreciative, stupid, spoiled, too impressed with his graduate education. 'I,' said the father, 'control this company. And tomorrow I am going to fire my son as president. The company has not made the progress it should have since I gave him the reins, and I am needed now to salvage what I can. All that Mother and I have in the world is tied up in this company, and we can't stand by idly and watch it go down the drain.' At the climax of a series of these wild statements, the father clutched his hands to his chest and slowly sank into his favorite chair, giving all the impressions of a heart attack. The event did serve to calm him down, and soon we were able to have a reasonably sensible and non-emotional conversation.

"I think that during the ten years I served that company as a director, the son was fired twenty-three times, and I, as his school classmate and accomplice, was fired about fifteen times."

This example, presented at some length, was typical of many family situations studied. Others could be described, but they would be repetitious of the same theme. In some, the possible contributions of outside board members were not realized because the controlling family owners wanted on the board only a limited number of family representatives. In others, outside board members mutually acceptable to the various family owners were unable to reconcile the differences of judgment which arise in every business organization. In other situations, outside board members *did* serve as conciliators, arbitrators, and resolvers of conflicts and problems.

It was found that the role of the outsider in these situations was delicate and difficult. Family members may rant and rave at and about each other. But the outsider must be most discreet in agreeing or disagreeing with intemperate statements made by one family member about another. The ties of family loyalty are exceedingly deep, blood is really thicker than water, and the unwary outside director can learn too late that identification with one side or the other may lead to disqualification and the end of his possible usefulness to family problems.

Relatively straightforward business problems sometimes become in family companies essentially emotional problems of the family members involved. The underlying—and fundamental—locus and quality of emotions are usually disguised with wide arrays of apparently logical and sensible statements by the participants. The problem of the outside director is to discern the real from the unreal, the emotion from the logic, and the motivation and aspirations of the family members involved. The task is not easy and is frequently frustrating. While occasionally directors found it to be most satisfying, others of those interviewed who served as directors of family companies, large and small, had concluded that the distinctive problems of directors of family enterprises were so laden with nonbusiness, non-administrative, and interlaced emotions that under no circumstances would they ever accept directorships on family boards again.

DIRECTORS AS DECISION MAKERS

In addition to serving as sources of advice and counsel, and as conciliators and arbitrators of family executives, board members of most family corporations perform two other functions described earlier for large and medium-sized companies: namely, serving as some sort of discipline for the management, and designating a replacement for the president in the event of a crisis such as his death or incapacity. In most of the family situations studied, the role of the directors did not include determining company objectives, strategies, and board policies; asking discerning questions; or selecting and evaluating the performance of the president.

A few situations were found, however, in which board members of family companies did in fact fulfill what has been described as the classic and generally accepted description of the responsible board functions.

• In one, for example, the president was head of a family enterprise started fifty years ago by his father and uncle. Ownership of the company stock was entirely in the hands of members of the family until 1965, when a public issue reduced the family holdings to 23 percent of the total. Of the 23 percent owned by various family members, approximately 15 percent was owned by the president, his wife, and two sons.

When the corporation was owned entirely by family members, the board had consisted of five directors from the family, plus the company legal counsel, who also served as legal counsel for the family. Over the years a variety of pleasure-serving assets were acquired by the company, primarily for the benefit of the family, and secondarily for the entertainment and service of company customers. Among these were a ten-place customized two-engine airplane, a 50-foot cabin cruiser based in the

Caribbean, a duck-hunting club off the East Coast, and a three-bedroom suite in a New York luxury hotel.

In what was found to be an unusual and atypical move, the president, prior to the public issue, sold the company airplane, cabin cruiser, and hunting camp, and cancelled the lease on the company suite in New York. In addition he decided that the company's new board of directors should be made up of outsiders except for the president. As board members, he invited the executive vice president of a commercial bank, the president of a large consumer products company, a senior partner of an investment banking firm, the head of a consulting firm specializing in marketing, and the president of a medium-sized manufacturing company.

Board meetings were held six times a year, and usually lasted all day. The president wanted involvement by the outsiders, and provided extensive and complete reports prior to meetings, to enable directors to study problems before they were discussed at the board meetings.

The president stated: "When the company was owned entirely by our family, I could live with the extravagance of the airplane and all our entertainment facilities. But when we have a bunch of outside stockholders I cannot in good conscience continue to enjoy these luxuries essentially paid for by somebody else. Before, it was our money, but now it is largely other people's money. I decided also that while I continued to control the enterprise with only 15 percent of the stock (our family name has been associated with the company for so many years I was sure that the new stockholders would go along with whatever I concluded was best for the company), I wanted independent outside board members to do a real job as responsible representatives for all the stockholders, not just the family. So I kicked off the board all the insiders and the company's legal counsel, and invited outsiders from a variety of companies and experiences. And for the first time in my life, I got turned down by the board.

"For example, one of our divisions had sales of over $100 million per year. About three years ago I brought in a new division manager from the outside. The first year the division sales and profits continued on the previous upward trend, but the last two years they have turned down. Sales were steady, but the profits just are not coming through. The division manager, his wife, and two children have become close personal friends of my family—I guess our wives talk to each other at least once a day, play golf together, and go shopping in New York together. During the last six months the board has been increasingly critical of the division results. Other companies in the same industry are doing fine, but we are not. At the end of a recent board meeting—I think it came under the heading of 'other business'—the outside board members and I discussed the performance of the division in my office—not in the board room—and they concluded that the main problem was the division manager. He had taken no perceptible steps to increase profitability, and the board could not perceive any program to recover market position. So as a group they decided the division manager must be terminated.

"This was really a tough one. I had hired him three years ago to run the division. At first, as the board members talked about his results, I defended him, saying, 'Give him another six months, and then let's look at his performance.' But they were firm and insistent that he be replaced immediately. That night I told my wife about the board's conclusion, and she was shocked. That whole complex of involved inter-family relations would be shattered, undoubtedly, if the division manager were terminated. There was much pillow talk that night. But the next morning we held a special meeting of the board, with the division manager, and he was permitted to resign. Emotionally I did not want to take this action, and my wife Shirley did not want to. But there it is. I am sure I could have overruled the board. But if I had, that would have been the end of that board's continued and interested involvement."

• An outside director of another family company stated: "I have been a director of the company for seven years. The chairman and president are brothers who built the business to a sales volume of over $200 million per year, and with a steadily improving earning trend. I came on the board when the company went public, and today, of the eleven board members, the only insiders are the chairman and the president. The traditional market for the company's product is flattening out, and also it is looking more and more like a commodity market where price is the main element of competition. Recently we had the opportunity to acquire a large vending-machine company which distributed cigarettes, candy, gum, and coffee through the machines. But 80 percent of their volume was in cigarettes. The two top executives and their staff had studied the opportunity carefully, and at a board meeting last year we spent most of one day reviewing and discussing the staff study on the company, which recommended that we purchase the enterprise.

"We went round and round. Management wanted the company, and a few directors agreed with the management, but other directors concluded that it would be a great mistake to jeopardize the company's image by being in a business that promoted the use of cigarettes—you know, the big to-do about cigarettes and health. The VP of planning countered by stating that we would *not* be directly identified with cigarettes, because the vending-machine company would maintain its own corporate identity and would be an autonomous profit and loss measurable entity. There was just no consensus, so the chairman suggested we all think about it for two weeks, and then we would have a special meeting of the board. We reassembled, and the previous positions were essentially reaffirmed.

"The chairman decided that with such a major commitment at stake, and with a segment of the board—though not a majority—convinced that the company's prestige in the industry would be tarnished by promoting the sale of cigarettes, the company should forgo the opportunity to acquire the vending-machine company. Here was a classic example of family top executives looking to the board for involvement in major decisions, and expecting the board to make decisions in the company's interest. But everybody on the board knows that the family control permits the chairman and the president to overrule the board. I should say in passing that if it were not this way, I wouldn't stay on the board. Last year I resigned from the board of another family company because I was convinced that the new president, the son of the chairman, intended not to follow the example of his father. For example the new president, without consulting the board, moved the company headquarters to another city because that was where he wanted to live."

GEOGRAPHICAL LIMITATIONS

It was found that among family-controlled corporations it was relatively rare that the president regarded boards of directors as anything more than sources of advice and counsel, even in large and medium-sized companies with non-family stockholders owning over 90 percent of the shares outstanding. To assure compliance and nondissent from members of the board, many family company presidents, it was found, choose only insiders or top executives from the city or region where the company headquarters is located.

• For example, an outside director of a large family-controlled company in New Orleans stated: "This board is a good example of a family enterprise. There are eleven members, with an executive committee of the board consisting of five. The five are the chairman, his older son as vice chairman, his younger son as president, and then the vice president of finance, and the vice president who is general counsel. The executive committee of the board also serves as the operating management committee of the company. The other six members of the board include two former insiders now retired, the retired president of a large New Orleans bank, a partner of the company's New Orleans legal counsel, the retired president of a New Orleans public utility, and the management partner of a brokerage firm in New Orleans.

"The board meets once a month, usually with one month missed a year. The outside board members, as you can see, are all local, so it is easy to get together for board meetings. The meetings don't last very long, like an hour, and the board members listen to a very brief, almost cursory, review of operations. And what the board does can be summarized very simply: practically nothing.

"All the board members are either insiders, former insiders (retired vice presidents), or active or retired presidents of local companies. These men are old friends and cronies of the old man, and about as provincial as you can be. Individually, the men on the board are some damn good people, but you can forecast that they will go along with anything that the old man wants. New Orleans is an out-of-the-way place, and although the company does a national and international business, the company headquarters is in New Orleans and strongly oriented to that area. If the board included members even from, say, Houston, which is very close, the breadth of point of view would be increased. But the chairman does not want what you might call positive influences. He's got the kind of board he wants, and he thinks it's just fine."

• "I was an outside board member of a family company. Its sales almost reached $1 billion, and the company had been very successful during the generation of the chairman. The headquarters were in Atlanta, and I was one of two outsiders of a board membership of twelve—the other outsider was a partner of a large New York investment banking firm. The rest of the board consisted of pseudo- or quasi-retired members of the family who had offices and secretaries at the headquarters but no positions of responsibility, the head of a large local law firm, inside executives, and a few local company presidents. The outside legal counsel, who was also the family's legal counsel, had drawn various trust instruments for the founder of the company, now dead, and was a trustee of some of the family's trusts. The role of the board was perfectly clear: attend quarterly meetings, vote yes when requested, don't ask any questions, and draw your fees. The board was designed and manned to act as subservient agents of the family management. Can you reasonably expect the company and family legal counsel to challenge the family that largely supports him? Can you reasonably expect the New York investment banker to take positions contrary to the president's, and thereby risk losing the company's account? I thought the direction of the company was questionable, and when I raised doubts about where the company seemed to be going, the president asked me to resign."

SELECTION OF PRESIDENT'S SUCCESSOR

I reported earlier that in most large companies the board of directors does not, except in a narrow legal sense, select the president's successor. Rather in most cases the president chooses which person inside or outside the company will be the next chief executive officer. In family-controlled corporations, whether small, medium, or large, the top family respresentative typically chooses who shall be president, and the board typically performs the ministerial legal ritual of confirming the family's decision. The situation is very much like the large companies described earlier—but with one important difference, it was found.

When, in a family company situation, the controlling family member president decides that his successor should be his son, or brother, or son-in-law, or some blood or married relation, the outside director is generally confronted with a genuine problem. Most fathers, I found, are incapable of appraising objectively the qualifications and desires of a son or sons working in family enterprises. It is probably not surprising, but fathers, as heads of family companies, in some cases aided and counseled by mothers, were found to identify virtues and skills where none existed; to perceive interest in and devotion to careers in business and the family company where sons manifestly wanted out; and to assume that their perceptions about their sons must be shared by anyone not blind to facts, and not stupid or intransigeant.

• The director of one large family company stated: "This company was put together in the late 1920s by the retired chairman. He was a great entrepreneur and literally designed the dimensions of the company and managed it to a great success. In the early 1940s he stepped aside as chief executive officer, and with his son just out of college and starting work as a company salesman, selected a nonfamily insider as president. That decision, I have been told, was warmly endorsed by the members of the board—inside and outside members alike.

"In the early 1950s the president was due to retire, and the chairman asked him to poll the directors on their judgments as to who should be the next president. By this time the chairman's son was in his middle thirties and had progressed to become manager of one of the company's smaller operating divisions. Without exception the directors reported to the president that one of two top nonfamily executives should be named president; and when the chairman's son's name was suggested by the president, all outside directors expressed convictions that he was too young, and too inexperienced, although highly motivated to get the job. Later that year when the president retired, the chairman advised members of the board individually that his son had demonstrated top executive abilities in his job as division manager, that he was highly motivated to do as well as his father, and that he should be named as president. He was. And for eight years the company went downhill. The chairman died, and the son, with some pressure from the board, went outside the company and selected and hired a professional manager. That chairman saw himself in the son, and no amount of logic could possibly overcome those convictions."

• "The chairman of the company where I was president has three sons in the business, and he thinks they are great executives because they agree with what he says and decides. I came into the family company when they acquired the enterprise I headed. The chairman of the acquiring company, and now of the combined companies, was one of the really great entrepreneurs of his generation. He built up a very successful business through internal growth, and then more than doubled its size and profits by acquiring the company where I was president. The chairman, his three sons, and I ostensibly ran the company, but in reality the chairman called the shots. The sons are in their early forties, and about two years apart in age. Each is independently wealthy in that their father gave them company stock when they were very young and when the stock had virtually no value.

"And the three sons are quite different. One majored in physics in college; he would like to add a Ph.D. to his Master's degree and then teach in some university. Another has a boat in Florida and would like to spend the rest of his life fishing. Intellectually he is the brightest one of the lot. The third is the least bright of the three, and wants to make a career in the family business. Today all three occupy top positions in the company, and their father believes without any question that they will carry on the family tradition as a hard-working team of three, after he has gone to his reward. I am convinced that when the father dies, son number one will get his Ph.D., son two will go fishing, and son three will run and wreck the company. That is why I resigned."

• "When I went on the board of a family company, the president told me that his twin thirty-year-old sons were extremely able, chips off the old block, and dedicated to continuing the heritage and tradition of the family's leadership of an enterprise now 80 percent owned by nonfamily members. During the next few years I became a good friend of the two sons and an admirer of their imagination and intellect. But as I came to know them better and share their interests and aspirations, it became clearer and clearer that what they wanted to do more than anything else in the world was to get out of business. One wanted to return to his prep school as a teacher of English and the drama. The other wanted to travel, write poetry, and paint. Their father was completely unaware of these carefully disguised and concealed feelings. At a board meeting I asked the sons, 'Do you really want to run this company for the next five years and for the rest of your lives?' The sons hesitated and then almost in unison said, 'No. I don't really want to devote my life to business.' The father was startled, shocked, amazed, incredulous. This was the first disclosure by his sons that the father's dream of continued leadership by family members would not be fulfilled. Over the next several months the chairman became reconciled to his sons' position, and, being the tough-minded old codger that he is, decided that the best solution would be to sell the enterprise to an attractive acquirer. He negotiated the sale of the company, and one son is now a school teacher at his prep school and the other is writing poetry in Spain. The father thought he knew his children, but it took over thirty years for him to discover what they were really like."

Many examples of similar situations were found in which fathers of family-controlled companies were unable to appraise objectively the abilities of their sons, and were unaware of the sons' personal ambitions and desires. Directors outside the family have the difficult and almost impossible task of suggesting to able but emotionally involved fathers that there might be better candidates for the presidency than the father's son. This is a distinctive problem of the board of directors of a family-controlled company.

Personal Services to Family Members

Another distinctive problem is that many family enterprises, when owned completely by one or a few families, frequently serve as legal vehicles for the provision of personal services, conveniences, or luxuries at company expense. When a company is completely owned by a family, the main party at interest, besides the family members who enjoy the benefits, is the Internal Revenue Service. But when the family enterprise becomes a family-controlled enterprise with extensive stockholdings by nonfamily shareholders, an additional party of interest is added—namely, the nonfamily shareholders.

It was found that in many family companies the change from family-owned to family-controlled status with new outside stockholders had little effect on the means employed to serve the convenience of the family members inside and outside the employ of the company. Company aircraft continued to be used by family members, including wives, to commute to summer or winter retreats. Limousines and apartments were maintained for business and nonbusiness purposes. Salaries, bonuses, and entertainment expenses were maintained on the same basis as when the family owned the entire company. And household and garden help continued to be on the corporate payroll as maintenance personnel for the company.

It is extremely difficult for a nonfamily director to be, or to become, aware of the extent to which company assets are, or have been, diverted to the personal benefit of family members. Any questions raised by an interested and responsible director suggest doubt as to the integrity of the family management—a doubt which, if expressed, is regarded as improper and inappropriate for a director. This is a common dilemma for the responsible outside director serving on boards of family companies: "Do I raise the question and thereby jeopardize my relations with the family president, or do I remain silent and assume that the benefits are not excessive, that the IRS will keep them within reasonable limits, that the company and family counsel must be aware of the legal implications, and that with these safeguards I do not have to worry about fulfilling my responsibilities to stockholders outside the family?"

CONCLUSIONS

What boards of directors do in family corporations is determined not only by what those members of the family with powers of control permit the boards to do, but also by the underlying and fundamental psychological distinctive characteristics of family enterprises. These psychological factors of family relationships constitute the extra ingredient which profoundly influences what directors do or do not do. Observations perfectly normal and straightforward by a director in a large company would be abnormal and inappropriate in a family corporation. The existence and involvement of the family makes the situation different from that of the nonfamily company

It was found, for example, that in family-controlled corporations the board of directors does serve as sources of advice and counsel, but the advice and counsel are deemed to be primarily for the benefit of the family. If a member of the family is president, the directors' advice was found to be useful to the president. But if the family members in control of the company have employed a nonfamily professional manager as president, the directors' advice-and-counsel role then was deemed to be primarily for the benefit of the family group, and secondarily for the nonfamily president. Generally it was found that dominant family members communicated to the outside-the-family board members that one of their important roles was to advise the family of their opinions of the company.

It was found that directors of family enterprises, in addition to serving as sources of advice and counsel to the family, served as arbitrators and conciliators in helping to resolve the high-emotion crisis issues sometimes encountered in family situations. The conflicts, rivalries, guilt feelings, ambitions, loyalties, prides, resentments, and interrelationships of family members in the same organization inevitably result in controversies which mature and skillful outside directors can, and do, help resolve. In a few cases, of course, the emotional problems of the various family members are remediable only through a professional psychological consultant. My own experiences suggest that these situations are no place for the efforts of a well-meaning amateur. It was found, however, that a contribution could be made by interested and involved outside directors to other problems.

Because of family suspicions, it was found to be extremely important for the outside director to maintain the utmost calm and objectivity under the tension and stress perpetrated by emotional family combatants. Family business differences and quarrels are distinctive from differences and quarrels encountered in nonfamily companies. In family companies members of the group feel privileged, and it seems in some cases almost obligated, to be as personally offensive and insulting as possible. Comments below any respectable standard of social behavior are exchanged among family members, and it is the wise director who hears but does not visibly react, and who restrains from approving or disapproving the points made by any of the participants. Blood—for those who have not served as directors of family corporations—*is* thicker than water. One effective way of unifying the antagonistic members of a family business conflict is for the nonfamily director to be critical or disapproving of the behavior of some member of the family. While this is an effective device for the reunification of feuding family business executives, the outside director may find the price high in that the usual next step is that he is asked to resign from the board.

In family-controlled companies the selection and deselection of corporation presidents typically was found to be made by the dominant representative of the family in control of the company. It was found that fathers generally —especially entrepreneurial-type company-founding fathers —are incapable of making an objective evaluation of the qualifications of their sons or relatives as candidates for the position of president. In some cases the members of the board were able to advise and counsel the dominant family member, but in most cases the decision-making power was in the family members, whether they were numerically in the majority on the board or not.

As was the case in large companies, there were a few

family-controlled companies in which the dominant family member chose to treat the enterprise like a publicly held company, and to regard the board of directors as the controlling layer of top management. In these situations the board of directors did, in fact, select, appraise, and evaluate the president; determine corporate objectives, strategies, and broad policies; ask discerning questions; and perform the other advisory and discipline roles. But, again, these situations were rare.

CHAPTER IX

Conclusions

B OARDS of directors have been part of our business scene
for over 150 years, but their functions have not been
clearly defined and generally accepted through practice in
the management of corporations. The provisions of the
general corporation law, "The business of a corporation
shall be managed by a board of at least three directors,"
and hundreds of judicial opinions written on legal issues
involving directors, provide no consistent and useful definitions of what directors' functions are. There is an abun-
dance of business literature attempting to define appropriate
roles for boards, but these efforts, while slightly less general
than the phrase "shall manage," do not describe with useful
precision what boards should do.

As I served on and worked with boards of directors, it
became clear that there was a considerable gap between
what directors in fact do and what the business literature
said they should do. My research work and this report were
efforts to determine what directors really do and to measure
the gap between the myths of business literature and the
realities of business practice.

WHAT DIRECTORS DO

In most companies boards of directors serve as a source
of advice and counsel, serve as some sort of discipline, and
act in crisis situations if the president dies suddenly or is

asked to resign because of unsatisfactory management performance.

Advice and Counsel

It was found that most presidents and outside board members agree that the role of directors is largely advisory and not of a decision-making nature. Management manages the company, and board members serve as sources of advice and counsel to the management. Also most presidents exploit the sources of advice represented on the board, both at board meetings and outside as well. And some thoughtful presidents, when selecting new members of the board to fill vacancies, identify the particular sets of desired qualities or areas of advice—general or specialized—which the presidents believe will add something to their management decisions.

Since typically directors do not devote substantial amounts of time to the affairs of the companies they serve, their advice cannot be of the sort which requires lengthy and penetrating analysis. Accustomed, however, to dealing with top management problems involving sums of money and financial implications of considerable magnitude, directors, within the time constraints, can provide useful inputs to presidents willing to listen.

Outside directors were found to be especially helpful in the advisory role where their general or specialized backgrounds and experiences could be applied to the specific management problems of the company served. For example, if new loans are to be negotiated, or if new financing is to be arranged, these are the kinds of problems commonly faced by those on the board, and their judgments on interest rates or terms are useful to the president. Or if the management of a company's pension plan is under review, the experience of other top executives is another bit of useful evidence for the president working for a solution. And if a new plant location, domestic or abroad, is involved in a request for a capital appropriation, members of the board with similar recent experience can often suggest useful and sometimes new factors bearing on the decision to commit large amounts of capital to a specific location. Occasionally, but not frequently, the advice and counsel of a board member leads to a reconsideration or a modification of a management's commitment or decision. Occasionally, but very rarely, the advice and counsel of a board member lead to a reversal of a management commitment or decision.

Some Sort of Discipline

A second role performed by boards of directors is serving as some sort of discipline for the president and his subordinate management. The president and his subordinates know that periodically they must appear before a board made up largely of their peers. It was found that even in those situations where managements know from previous experience that members of the board will not ask penetrating, discerning, and challenging questions, considerable care is taken in preparing figures and reports for board meetings. Something in the way of discipline results simply from the fact that regular board meetings are held.

Presidents and other members of management, in describing the discipline value of boards, indicated that the requirement of appearing formally before a board of directors consisting of respected, able people of stature, no matter how friendly, causes the company organization to do a better job of thinking through their problems and of being prepared with solutions, explanations, or rationales.

The discipline value of boards was found to serve as an

administrative device for presidents to use in establishing standards of performance for work done by subordinates. With capital appropriations on the agenda for the next board meeting, many presidents remind functional or divisional managers that market and financial justifications have to be carefully organized and documented so that there will be no possibility of embarrassing questions from board members.

As an element of the discipline concept described by those interviewed, some used the phrase "corporate conscience." The board of directors is regarded as the guardian to assure, and to represent to the outside world, that the president and his subordinates do not engage in what might be regarded by outsiders as unconscionable conduct. The establishment of a compensation and stock option committee, for example, consisting entirely of outside directors with the president serving as an ex officio member, is assurance, at least theoretically, that compensation policies and practices do not exceed the appropriate bounds of reasonableness.

Usually the symbols of corporate conscience are more apparent than real, and presidents with complete powers of control make the compensation policies and decisions. The compensation committee, and the board which approves the recommendations of the compensation committee, are not in most cases decision-making bodies. These decisions are made by the president, and in most situations the committee and board approval is perfunctory. The president has de facto powers of control, and in most cases he is the decision maker. The board does, I believe, tend to temper the inclinations of presidents with de facto control, and it does contribute to the avoidance of excesses. Thus it serves the important role of a corporate conscience.

Decision Making in Crisis Situations

There are two crisis situations where the role of the board of directors is more than advisory. First, if the president dies suddenly or becomes incapacitated, the board has the responsibility to select his successor. In some cases the selection process is largely controlled by the deceased president who has discussed with board members what he wanted them to do "if he is hit by a truck some day." In other instances board members and presidents have neglected to consider the problem of succession. Only when confronted with the unexpected death of the president have they been propelled into a decision-making function. But the board is there—legally constituted to pick a successor and to ensure the continuity of an entity organized to operate in perpetuity.

The drama and trauma that develop when a board of directors has thrust upon it unexpectedly the complete de facto powers of control were illustrated during many of the interviews. The dynamics of the assumption of all or part of the de facto powers of control by individual directors and combines of directors is worthy, in my judgment, of a separate study.

The second crisis situation in which the board of directors performs a decision-making role is when leadership and performance of the president are so unsatisfactory that a change must be made. Here the president is asked to resign—an important decision. And then the board must decide upon a successor—an equally important decision.

I have concluded that generally boards of directors do not do an effective job of evaluating or measuring the performance of the president. Rarely are standards or criteria established and agreed upon by which the president can be measured other than the usual general test of corporate profitability, and it is surprising how slow some directors are to respond to years of steadily declining profitability. Since directors are selected by the president, and group and individual loyalties have been developed through working together, directors are reluctant to measure the executive performance by the president carefully against specific standards. Directors base their appraisals largely on data and reports provided by the president himself. Also, top executives serving as outside directors, being exceedingly busy men, typically do not devote the time to pursue through further inquiry any concerns they may deduce from the data presented to them as directors, even when the concern might extend to the performance of the president.

In those situations where mounting and persuasive evidence leads individual directors or groups of directors to a conclusion that the president is unsatisfactory, it was found that one of three courses of action is usually followed:

(1) *Hire a management consultant.* Periodic management audits by consulting firms appear to be increasingly common and accepted by top executives even in highly successful enterprises. Employing consultants to identify problems at the president's level and to recommend changes, it was found, is used as a means of handling discreetly the unpleasant task of communicating to a president that he is inadequate.

(2) *Resign from the board.* This is the most common and typical response of directors who suspect or conclude that the president is unsatisfactory. Resignation from boards for plausible reasons such as conflict of interest enables a director to avoid facing the ultimate and inevitably unpleasant task of acting to replace a president. In addition, with public disclosure of an apparently reasonable basis for a resignation, typically there is no embarrassment to the company or to the believed-to-be-inadequate president.

(3) *Ask the president to resign.* Most boards of directors and most individual directors are intensely reluctant to face the

unpleasant conclusion that the president of the company must be terminated. While sometimes the unpleasantness is avoided by hiring outside consultants or by resigning from the board, there are some situations in which board members who have procrastinated in taking any action find themselves obligated to face the task of asking the president to resign. These situations were found to be relatively rare.

In these cases where the board assumed an important decision-making role by asking for the president's resignation, I found that board members were impressive in their ability and their willingness to assume top corporate responsibilities measured by any set of standards. For the most part the outside directors remained on the board and devoted more than casual amounts of time to the company in distress. Many directors expressed regret for not having responded to the symptoms of weakness they had seen earlier, now more recognizable than before. Finally having faced the issue of the president's shortcomings, however, they stayed on the board even though it would have been less embarrassing not to be identified with a company with top management problems. They gave more of their time to the affairs of the ailing company, and they acted as responsible corporate citizens by assuming for the interim the de facto powers of control held previously by the president.

WHAT DIRECTORS DO NOT DO

The business literature describing the classical functions of boards of directors typically includes three important roles: (1) establishing basic objectives, corporate strategies, and broad policies; (2) asking discerning questions; and (3) selecting the president.

Establishing Objectives, Strategies, and Policies

I found that boards of directors of most large and medium-sized companies *do not* establish objectives, strategies, and policies, however defined. These roles are performed by company managements. Presidents and outside directors generally agreed that only management can and should have these responsibilities.

The determination of a company's objectives, strategies, and direction requires considerable study of the organization's strengths and weaknesses and its place in the competitive environment, careful, time-consuming, penetrating analysis of market opportunities, and a matching of the organizational capacities to meet and serve the changing requirements of the market. And the market, for more and more companies, includes opportunities abroad, thus adding another complicating dimension of analysis. The typical outside director does not have time to make the kinds of studies needed to establish company objectives and strategies. At most he can approve positions taken by management, and this approval is based on scanty facts and not time-consuming analysis.

Giving operational meaning to a set of defined corporate objectives is usually achieved by allocating or re-allocating corporate capital resources. Statements of objectives and strategies are merely products of an analytical exercise until steps are taken to modify or redirect the company's activities through new allocations of corporate capital. The managements of a few companies, it was found, do not accept the idea that boards can or should be involved in the process of capital appropriations, even in an advisory capacity. Accordingly, studies and approvals of capital appropriations are made at management levels and not at the level of the board of directors.

In most companies the allocation of capital resources, including the acquisition of other enterprises, is accomplished through a management process of analysis resulting in recommendations to the board and in requests for approval by the board. The minimum dollar amounts which require board approval and the amount of analytical supporting data accompanying the requests vary among companies. Approval by boards in most companies is perfunctory, automatic, and routine. Presidents and their subordinates, deeply involved in analysis and decision making prior to presentation to the board, believe in the correctness of their recommendations and almost without exception they are unchallenged by members of the board. Rarely do boards go contrary to the wishes of the president.

In a few instances boards of directors do establish objectives, strategies, and major policies, but these are exceptions. Here the president wants the involvement of directors and not only allows but insists on full discussion, exploration of the issues, agreement, and decision by the board along with the president.

Asking Discerning Questions

A second classical role ascribed to boards of directors is that of asking discerning questions—inside and outside the board meetings. Again it was found that directors *do not,* in fact, do this. Board meetings are not regarded as proper forums for discussions arising out of questions asked by board members. It is felt that board meetings are not intended as debating societies.

Many board members cited their lack of understanding of the problems and the implications of topics that are presented to the board by the president, and to avoid "looking like idiots" they refrain from questions or comments.

Presidents generally do not want to be challenged by the questions of directors, especially if subordinates of the president are on the board or attending the meeting. It was found that most presidents profess that they want questions asked by interested members of the board, but I concluded that while they say this and even go to some trouble to make directors feel that they are free to do so, actually the presidents do not want questioning or comment. The unsophisticated director may learn from experiencing rebuffs that presidents do not want penetrating, issue-provoking questions but only those which are gentle and supportive and and an affirmation that the board approves of him. Many presidents stated that board members should manifest by their queries, if any, that they approve of the management. If a director feels that he has any basis for doubts and disapproval, most of the presidents interviewed believe that he should resign.

The lack of active discussion of major issues at typical board meetings and the absence of discerning questions by board members result in most board meetings resembling the performance of traditional and well-established, almost religious, rituals. In most companies it would be possible to write the minutes of a board meeting in advance. The format is always the same, and the behavior and involvement of directors are completely predictable—only the financial figures are different.

Not many exceptions to this were found. A few presidents do, in fact, want discerning, challenging questions and active discussion of important issues at the board meetings. They think of the board as accountable and responsible to the company's owners. There are also a few directors who do in fact ask discerning questions notwithstanding the desires of the president.

Typical garden-variety outside directors, selected by the president and generally members of a peer group, do not ask questions inside or outside of board meetings. However, directors who serve on corporate boards of companies because they own or represent the ownership of substantial shares of stock generally do in fact ask discerning questions. Their willingness to query presidents is in part a manifestation of the split in the de facto powers of control of the companies. The large stockholder-directors are not usually on the board because the president wants them there, but because, through cumulative voting procedures, they can force their way onto the board.

Directors as described in the literature represent the stockholders. Yet typically they are actually selected by the president and not by the stockholders. Accordingly the directors are on the board because the president wants them there. Implicitly, and frequently explicitly, the directors in point of fact represent the president. But a large stockholder-director is not selected by the president and does not therefore represent the president; rather he represents himself and an interest more likely to be consistent with that of the other stockholders. The attitude of the large stockholder-director generally is: "This is my money—these are my assets." The attitude of the outside nonstockholder-director usually is: "This is somebody's else's money—these are not my assets." These differing attitudes with regard to stock ownership often are manifested in the extent to which discerning questions are asked of the president by the directors.

Selecting the President

A third classical role usually regarded as a responsibility of the board of directors is the selection of the president. Yet it was found that in most companies directors do not in fact select the president except under the two crisis situations cited earlier. In some situations formal or informal committees of outside members of boards are charged with the responsibility of evaluating candidates inside the management for the presidency. But generally these committees have no more control over the naming of the president than do similar committees charged with identifying and recommending the names of candidates for board membership. In both committee situations the president with de facto powers of control essentially makes the decisions. The administrative use by the president of board committees to evaluate candidates for his successor in the presidency gives the selection process an appearance of careful evaluation and objectivity. But in most cases the decision as to who should succeed the president is made by the president himself.

Certainly the president knows the key members of his organization better than anyone else. He has worked with them closely and typically over considerable periods of time. He has observed them under various conditions of stress and he, far better than anyone else on the board, can judge and predict which of the inside candidates can best fit the essentially unique set of job requirements of the company's presidency.

Board members with relatively brief exposure to company executives—whether on the board or not—base their appraisals necessarily on very inadequate evidence. When insiders appear before the board for presentations of their divisional operations, for example, or to explain a request for a large capital appropriation, the setting is artificial and synthetic. Executives, aware that the process of evaluation is going on, rehearse their appearances to communicate to the board that they have the capacities and skills needed for the presidency. And the most that outside directors can conclude from such an exposure is: "The executive gave a well-organized presentation, he answered questions well, he spoke well, and he handled himself well."

Boards of directors were found to serve in an advisory role in the selection of a new president—in their capacity as a sort of corporate conscience. The process of electing a new president requires a vote by the board, and the president generally observes the amentities of corporate good manners by discussing his choice with individual members prior to the meeting. Rarely does a board of directors reject a candidate for the presidency who is recommended by the president.

THE POWERS OF CONTROL IN THE CORPORATION

What boards of directors do is determined in large part by the location of the powers of control of the company, and by how the holders of the powers of control choose to exercise those powers.

In the small family company the ownership of the stock and the management are identical. The powers of control are in the family owners, and what the board of directors does is determined by the owners. In my earlier study it was found that the board usually consists of the father (the founder), his wife, and the family attorney. The owner-managers of some small companies add outside directors to multiply the inputs to policy making, policy implementation, and day-to-day operating problems. The primary function of the outside directors is to provide a source of advice and counsel to the family owner-managers, and they do not serve in a decision-making role except in the case of the unforeseen death of the dominant family owner-manager. Even then, the real decision typically is made by his heirs. They have the authority to manage the enterprise, and the board is at most a legally required body which can be used for advice and counsel on management or family problems. The family owners determine what the board does or does not do.

At the opposite end of the spectrum is the large, widely held corporation in which typically the president and members of the board own little stock. Here the de jure powers of control are dispersed among thousands of owners—stockholders who are generally unorganized as owners, and essentially unorganizable. And yet the president, in the absence of control or influence by the owners of the enterprise, typically does have the de facto powers to control the enterprise, and with these powers of control it is the president who, like the family owner-managers in the small company, determines in large part what the board of directors does or does not do.

Between these two corporate situations there are many variations and combinations of centers of control, or ownership influences on control, of the company. Complete de facto control by the professional manager-president may be diminished or influenced by the presence on the board of a person who owns, or represents the ownership of, a substantial block of stock. In this case the president's de facto powers of control in determining what the board does or does not do may be affected by what the owners or owner-representatives regard as appropriate functions of board members. This may constitute a challenge to the president. It was found that many directors who own, or represent the ownership of, substantial numbers of shares of stock take a deep interest in the operations of the company, spend considerable time in learning the business, and insist on being involved in major company decisions. The degree of the president's de facto powers of control in these cases is affected by the involvement of company stock owners.

Some directors who own or represent the ownership of large numbers of shares were found to be passive, compliant, and not involved in major company problems, and the president's complete powers of control are not diminished or influenced. Analysis of the situations where substantial stockholdings are represented on the board produced no factors which make possible any reliable prediction of whether the stockholder-director will take an active and involved question-asking role. There is some evidence that if the owner of the stock had come into possession of it through his own efforts, such as an entrepreneur developing his own business and then selling it to a larger company for its shares, the acquired entrepreneur will take a very active role as a director of the acquiring company. If the outside director with large stockholdings is a second or third generation heir of an entrepreneur, his involvement as an active director is less likely.

Another situation where the president of a large or medium-sized company was found not to possess the full and complete de facto powers of control is where a retired president stays on as a member of the board. Then typically the outside board members have been selected and invited to the board by the retired president, not the new president. A similar complication of relationships was found to exist in the situation following the sudden death of the president where his successor is designated by the board of directors. The new president holds his position because the directors selected him—directors who were themselves selected by his predecessor. While the new president is demonstrating his capacities to head the enterprise, the outside directors generally share the powers of control of the company. In both cases, with the passage of time, and the designation by the new president of new directors who are *his* directors, the complete powers of control will flow back into the office of the president.

The dynamics of the distribution and flow of powers of control between and among the directors and the president is an appropriate and worthy area for further research. Generally it was found that when the president and the directors own only a little stock, the president possesses and exercises the complete powers of control of the enterprise.

In addition to the location of the powers of control, an important factor affecting what boards of directors do and do not do is *how* the powers of control are exercised by the holders of these powers.

It was found that most presidents are completely aware of their powers of control, but they choose to exercise them in a moderate manner acceptable to their peers on the board. The president communicates to *his* board members that he does indeed control the enterprise, and while this is usually done discreetly, it is understood and accepted by the directors. Many of them, as presidents of their own companies with board members of their own, thoroughly understand the existence and location of the powers of control.

Most presidents think of their directors essentially as a source of advice and counsel, both at the board meetings and outside the meetings. The topics on which advice and counsel are provided, of course, lie within the discretion of the president who determines what items appear on the board meeting agenda and who picks the circumstances under which he chooses to seek the assistance of directors outside the periodic board meetings. Most presidents are willing, it was found, to listen to, and to take into account, the constructive advisory suggestions of directors.

The cases where presidents are described as exercising their de facto powers of control in a moderate manner include most of the situations studied. A few cases were found, however—and these were dramatic exceptions—in which the manner of the president can be characterized as that of a tyrant. A few presidents regard their board as an unnecessary legal appendage and board meetings as bothersome interruptions of their busy day-to-day management of the company. Such presidents may try to reduce the number of time-wasting board meetings by having them quarterly rather than monthly. They may also, for example, make top management changes without concurrence by, or even coordination with, the board. Their disrespect for the board and board functions flaunts their powers of control rather unpleasantly.

Outside directors of tyrant-led companies stated that their willingness to continue in completely meaningless roles as directors is attributable to "my longstanding friendship with the president, for whom I have the greatest admiration," or, "This is a very large and successful company and there is a certain amount of prestige in being identified with it as a director," or "The perquisites are great; where else can I get a free winter vacation in the Caribbean, great duck hunting in the fall, and a company jet which picks me up for every board meeting?"

This tyrannical exercise of the powers of control by presidents was found to exist in a relatively few situations, and an equally small fraction of cases were found in which the president's manner was at the other extreme. Some presidents, but not many, are completely aware that they have de facto powers of control and that they can behave in their relationships with their board in any manner that they elect, but they choose to include the board as a major and important element in the management structure. Such a president accepts the classical concept that the board does indeed represent the stockholders and as the president he is only one man in the total organization; and he wants the involvement of outside directors in determining objectives, asking discerning questions, and appraising and evaluating his performance as president. In these situations usually the only insiders on the board are the president and the chairman. Of all the companies studied over the years, including the last two of full-time intensive field research, only a relatively small minority of instances were encountered where the president felt this way.

OTHER FACTORS AFFECTING WHAT BOARDS OF DIRECTORS DO

The Way Directors Are Selected

Directors are generally selected and invited to serve on the board by the president of the company. In some instances a nominating committee of the board is created to identify, screen, and recommend candidates for board membership, It was found, though, that even with the presumed objectivity of a committee of outside directors, the decision as to new members is made by the president.

Again it should be noted that if one or more existing directors own or represent the ownership of substantial stock, the president's de facto power to select new directors may be challenged. In these cases the stock-owning directors are interested in adding new directors of *their* choice, and the president is interested in new directors of *his* choice. Discussion and negotiation inevitably result in some sort of agreement on who should be added, and the balance of power issue continues.

The stockholders, of course, unless their holdings are substantial enough to assure representation on the board through the provisions of cumulative voting or to result in an invitation by the president to serve, play no part in the selection of directors to fill vacancies or in the nomination of directors' names to be included in the annual proxy statement.

Interview discussions on the topic of who makes a good director indicated that presidents in selecting directors for their companies regard the titles and prestige of candidates as of primary importance. Candidates are usually chosen who are in positions equal to those of the other board members, in companies of prestige equivalent to that of the company to be served. If existing board members are chair-

men and presidents of companies or senior partners of leading financial or legal firms, potential board members with
lesser titles are rarely considered. Newly elected company
presidents and newly elected university presidents and
deans of graduate schools, it was found, were surprised by
the sudden influx of invitations they received to become
board members of large and prestigious companies.

In addition to the qualifications of prestige titles in
prestige institutions—both business and academic—outside
directors are selected who are known as noncontroversial,
friendly, sympathetic, congenial, and understanders of the
system. Boat-rockers and wave-makers generally are not the
choice of presidents with de facto powers of control and
with freedom of choice as to who should serve on their
boards.

While most presidents prefer to include on their boards
only those who have appropriate titles and positions, there
are a few presidents who believe that the requirement of
prestige titles is not important. They want board members
who will participate in the management of the company.
Not surprisingly, these presidents are the same ones who
want board members who will help establish corporate
objectives, ask discerning questions, and evaluate the performance of the president.

Motivations for Serving as Directors

The fact that the top executives of companies, academic
officials, and leading partners of financial institutions and
law firms are exceedingly busy people makes it unlikely
that they can become deeply involved in another company's
problems. They are successful in their respective areas of
primary activity because they pay the price of almost complete devotion to the enterprises for which they are responsible. The top position of virtually all business organizations is a time-consuming responsibility. The result is that

most top executives devote only nominal amounts of time to serving as directors of other companies.

The principal forces found to motivate business executives to accept board membership are: (1) the opportunity to learn through exposure to other companies' operations something of value that might be useful in their own situations; and (2) the intangible prestige value of identification with well-known and prestigious companies, executives, and other directors.

With few exceptions, top executives who serve as directors of other companies are extraordinary men. The competitive process by which men get promoted through the various levels of business and other large organizations generally provides highly qualified leaders of enterprises. They have demonstrated capacities, skills, and abilities to head significant companies, and they have the qualities to serve as outstanding directors of other enterprises. What they do as directors, however, is determined by the company president with control over their selection. Most presidents do not want outside directors to become involved in their companies, and the selection of busy top executives of equally prestigious organizations insures that by the nature of their positions they will not have time to give more than nominal attention to the affairs of the company served as a director.

*   *   *   *   *

During my last twenty-five years of involvement and study of boards of directors, two critically important issues concerning board membership were identified, and executives who were interviewed during the current field research were asked to comment on them: (1) Should inside full-time employees, other than the chairman of the board and the president, serve on the board of directors? (2) Should members of investment banking firms serve as directors of other companies?

THE ISSUE OF INSIDE DIRECTORS

I found that most presidents, even with complete de facto powers of control, prefer to have substantial numbers of insiders on their boards of directors. Very few presidents with whom I have discussed the inside/outside directors' issue believe or follow the practice of having all outsiders on the board (other than the chairman or the president). Most of those interviewed had one or more retired former company executives on their boards, but in all cases they counted them as outsiders when calculating the inside/outside director ratio.

Many reasons were given for having substantial numbers of insiders on the board of directors:

(1) Insiders on the board are available for comment on the operations and problems for which they are responsible. If questions arise during a board meeting with regard to, say, a capital appropriation, the interested vice president-director can respond, thus expediting the processing of capital appropriations requiring board approval.

(2) Board membership is said to be good for morale, not only of the insiders on the board, but also of their subordinates whose aspirations can appropriately include future board membership for themselves.

(3) Membership on the board constitutes a form of intangible compensation—a reward.

(4) Insiders serving as directors are exposed to broader management points of view, thus contributing to their growth as executives. Value is found in having insiders learn through personal experience how the management process works at board level.

(5) By having key insiders on the board, outside directors, working with them, will be able to evaluate them in terms of their abilities to serve as president should the incumbent president die unexpectedly.

I believe that the reasons given for having insiders other than the chairman and the president on the board are largely rationalizations and specious. Most of the objectives cited can be accomplished through other means. The reason insiders are on boards of directors is that their presidents want them there. If the president with de facto control perceives the functions of the board to be a source of advice and counsel and some sort of discipline, but a decision-making body only in the event of a crisis, then the proportion of inside/outside directors is academic and essentially irrelevant. In these cases the presence of insiders only reduces the number of sources of outside advice. But for the president this is counterbalanced by the presence at meetings of a core of presumed-to-be-loyal supporters.

If the president perceives the role of the board to be the fullment of the three functions listed above, but if in addition he wants the board to represent the stockholders' interests by determining objectives, strategies, and policies, asking discerning questions, and selecting, evaluating, and measuring the president's performance—then it is apparent that there should be no insiders on the board other than the chairman and the president. The logical extension of this conclusion is, of course, that the board should be made up entirely of outsiders, and that the chairman and the president should not be on the board themselves.

No instances were found among the companies studied where all directors were outsiders.

THE ISSUE OF INVESTMENT BANKERS AS DIRECTORS

During the last decade there has been increasing discussion among interested participants and observers as to whether investment bankers should serve on boards of directors. Partners of investment banking firms constitute one of the larger sources of directors. My discussions with top executives, both before and during the two-year field research period, indicated clearly that the issue is regarded as timely and important. It was observed also that most of those interviewed expressed firm convictions as to whether investment bankers should or should not serve on boards. Rarely was there a middle ground.

It was found that investment bankers, by the nature of their business, are regarded as extremely valuable members of boards. On financial matters, investment bankers provide a complementary and a supplementary source of knowledge to the financial expertise within the company. Experienced investment bankers, involved on a daily basis, are aware of money rates nationally and internationally, money terms, and market conditions, and they can evaluate the market's reaction to proposed moves by the company. This kind of current substantive financial intelligence is regarded by most presidents as essential.

In addition, investment bankers, through exposure to many different companies in many different industries and regions, bring to company presidents and company boards of directors what one president described as "a treasury of information." Bankers, as they practice their profession, are collectors of information—they learn the problems faced and approaches followed by presidents of a substantial number of other companies. Thus investment bankers as directors were described as "great pollenizers"—they lift ideas from one company and deposit them in other companies.

But it was acknowledged by corporate presidents as well as by partners of investment banking firms that the essential professional financial skills and the general management pollenizing knowledge are available to company presidents whether representatives of investment banking firms are on the boards or not. Investment firms provide professional services the value of which does not depend upon board membership.

Two persuasive reasons for not having investment bankers on boards were found:

(1) An investment banker on a board generally restricts the president to the professional services of that one firm. A representative of a certain investment banking firm on a company's board serves as a signal to the outside world that a firm-client relationship exists. The result is that other bankers with potentially useful financial services are discouraged from approaching the president of the apparently captive company. This finding was also confirmed by investment bankers who were interviewed. It was generally agreed that their primary reason for serving as company directors is a business-getting device, and if they do not get the financial services business, there is no purpose in being on the company board.

Not only do investment banking firms differ with regard to their relative expertise among the many areas of operations, but also one investment firm will vary from time to time with regard to its staff expertise in a certain area. Thus the president of a company restricted to the services of one investment banking firm with changing qualifications is not necessarily able to procure the best professional services available at the time when they are needed.

It was also quite common to find company presidents referring to "the seat" of a certain investment firm on their board, and observing that over the years the firm continued to be represented even though its representatives changed.

Some presidents and investment bankers stated that presidents are not necessarily limited to the services of one investment banking firm if a representative is on the board. It was found, however, that generally the presence of a banker on a board results in that firm, and only that firm, providing whatever investment services are purchased by the company.

(2) A second reason—and I believe far more important—for not having investment bankers on boards is that if they represent a firm which does investment counseling, employs brokers, or controls or advises mutual funds, the investment banker director has an absolute, real, and disqualifying conflict of interest. As a director, the banker has access to information not

available at the same time to the public or to others in the financial community, and information on companies and their operations is an essential ingredient in the function of investment banking firms.

Investment bankers are sensitively aware of the conflicts of interest resulting from their board memberships, and banking firms generally establish a structure of paper rules of procedure and practice intended to separate valuable inside information secured by one partner from use by another partner in, say, the investment counseling area of the firm. These rules, in my judgment, are patently artificial and generally meaningless. It would be unreal to expect investment banking partners with a mutual interest in their firm's profits not even to talk with each other. Investment bankers, to carry that load of conflict without ever breaching the faith, would have to be more honest than people!

In addition to the conflict of interest arising out of information received as an insider, the investment banker-director has another form of conflict when he identifies a company for acquisition and participates in the negotiations resulting in acquisition. The professional and usually highly competent services of an investment banker in finding companies worthy of acquisition, and then in serving as an adviser on the financial terms of a contract to acquire a company, certainly deserve appropriate fees for the services performed. Typically the fees charged for professional work on acquisitions are a function of the monetary size of the acquisition, and also typically the payment of fees is contingent upon the completion of the acquisition—no acquisition, no fee. If a partner of an investment banking firm is a director of the acquiring company, the conflict of interest is apparent and real. Obviously the interests of his firm will be served through the fees paid for professional services if the identified candidate for acquisition is purchased. Some situations were found where the investment banker-director refrained from voting at the board meeting either on the acquisition or on the fees to be paid to his firm. This in my judgment is a meaningless gesture, in that the banker representative as a director is in a position of influence on the board of directors—an arm's-length relationship is inherently impossible.

I conclude that representatives of investment banking firms should not serve as members of corporate boards of directors.

BOARDS OF DIRECTORS IN FAMILY COMPANIES

This report has been concerned largely with what boards of directors of large and medium-sized companies in fact do. Reference was made earlier to the balance of powers of control in those situations where the de facto powers of the president were challenged or diminished by owners or representatives of owners of large blocks of stock. There is another distinctive group of companies known as family companies in which members of the boards of directors were found to have similar but different roles from those of directors in other companies.

The singular difference in family companies is that boards of directors operate in a working environment complicated by the psychological implications of family members working in the same organization—with and against each other. Members of a family bring into the business conflicts, rivalries, guilt feelings, ambitions, loyalties, prides, resentments, and interrelationships which are quite different from the characteristics of typical nonfamily companies.

Family members with de jure powers of control—or de facto powers if shares have been sold or traded to owners outside the family—determine what the boards of directors do or do not do. Board members, it was found, may be in the position of having to serve as arbitrators and conciliators on issues arising among family members in the company. These issues, many times with emotional extras added to the usual problems encountered in business operations, are amenable to compromise and solution by alert and discreet board members. It was found also that in most family company situations directors serve as sources of advice primarily to the family, and secondarily to the president if he is not a member of the family. Family owners generally want advice and counsel from directors bearing on, for example, the monitoring and measuring of the performance of the company president if he is not a family member, or on whether or how to sell the enterprise to which of several potential corporate acquirers. The controlling owners also seek advice and counsel on the same subjects as those for nonfamily companies.

Boards of directors serve as some sort of discipline for the president, but especially for nonfamily subordinates in the organization. But in contrast to large and medium-sized companies, boards generally do not select a successor if the president dies unexpectedly or is found to be unsatis-factory. This type of decision typically is made by members of the family who own or have inherited the ownership of the enterprise.

It was found also that in most family companies boards of directors do not determine corporate objectives, strate-gies, or general policies. Nor do they ask discerning ques-tions or evaluate the president if he is a family member. If he is not a family member but a professional manager, the owners in control want appraisals of the president by board members but reserve for themselves the decision-making power to terminate his employment.

Two unique problem areas confront directors of family companies:

(1) The inability of fathers in control of family enterprises to be objective in appraising the capacities, skills, and motivations of their sons. This is probably true of most fathers, but the frailty is especially relevant when the sons are candidates for the presidency of a family business organization. And this pre-sents an especially uncomfortable dilemma for the outside

director when the family in control owns a relatively small percentage of the stock and the balance is publicly owned.

(2) The use of company assets by controlling family members. Some family companies serve as legal vehicles for the provision of personal services, conveniences, and luxuries to family members at company expense. When the enterprise is owned completely by the family, the only other real party of interest and concern is the Internal Revenue Service, and its task turns on whether the costs are appropriate business expenses. But when the family company includes as stockholders people outside the family, another party of interest and concern is present. And the director has a problem: "Do I represent the family stockholders, or do I represent all the stockholders?"

The general conclusions on what directors do in most family companies must include mention of a few exceptional family companies where boards of directors do in fact determine objectives, strategies, and general policies; ask discerning questions; evaluate and measure the performance of the president whether he is a member of the family or not; provide advice and counsel; serve as some kind of discipline; and select and elect the president. These situations are rare.

SUMMARY OF FINDINGS

In a final summary of my study of directors, I found that in large and medium-sized companies where the president and board members own only a few shares of stock:

1. Presidents with de facto powers of control select the members of the boards.
2. Presidents determine what boards do and do not do.
3. Directors selected are usually heads of equally pres-

tigious organizations with primary responsibilities of their own.

4. Heads of businesses and financial, legal, and educational organizations are extremely busy men with limited motivation and time to serve as directors of other organizations.

5. Most boards of directors serve as advisors and counselors to the presidents.

6. Most boards of directors serve as some sort of discipline for the organization—as a corporate conscience.

7. Most boards of directors are available to and do make decisions in the event of a crisis.

8. A few boards of directors establish company objectives, strategies, and broad policies. Most do not.

9. A few boards of directors ask discerning questions. Most do not.

10. A few boards evaluate and measure the performance of the president and select and de-select the president. Most do not.

QUESTIONS POSED BY THESE FINDINGS

These conclusions pose questions and challenges to all those who are interested in business:

- If this is what directors do,

      —what, if anything, needs to be done?
                                    should be done?
                                       by whom?

- If this is what directors do,

      —is it enough?

- If the roles of the board are defined as:

      to provide advice and counsel,
      to serve as some sort of discipline,

to serve as a decision-making body in the event of a crisis,

—don't we need a new set of laws redefining the legal responsibilities of directors?

• If the roles of boards are defined so as to serve these three functions and

to determine objectives, strategies, and policies,
to ask discerning questions,
to evaluate and measure the president's performance,
to select and de-select the president,

—shouldn't directors spend a great deal more time as directors?
—is it possible to find competent men and women with the time and motivation to accept directorships with these requirements?
—should the president select directors charged with evaluating and measuring his own performance?
—do directors represent the president who selects them, or the stockholders who had nothing to do with their selection?
—who should select directors?

• Do investor-stockholders need a board of directors "to manage" the company?

• If directors are needed to comply with legal require-ments, why not have a board comprised of insiders only?

• Should not the board consist of *all* outsiders, and serve as a layer of management to which the president reports but of which he is not a member?

• What *should* boards of directors do?